Table of Conte

Forward

It has been said that a writer should write from his or her own experience. At seventy plus years, I have had plenty of experience. I have been a psychologist, musician, day laborer, researcher, teacher, education evaluator, computer programmer, database administrator, and statistician. I had intended to be a psychologist for my entire working life but "stuff happens". Like so many students, I was told to pick an occupation that I enjoyed, was good at, and would sustain me. I chose to be a psychologist. Unfortunately, there was something else to consider that seldom comes up when choosing an occupation - *Is this an occupation where merit counts?* In other words, do the best psychologists get chosen for jobs? Do the best psychologists advance? Do the best psychologists make the most money?

Choosing an occupation is one of the most important decisions a person makes in one's lifetime. Next to sleep, work will consume more of your time than any other activity. It is probably as important as choosing a spouse or where you would like to live. Most vocational counselors believe you should find an occupation that fits your interests, special talents, and ability/intelligence. Some people believe we have different types of intelligence such as verbal, spatial, mathematical, musical, and kinesthetic. Emotional intelligence includes reading body language and tone of voice to determine a person's emotions

Anne Roe, who developed a theory of career development, classified occupations into service, business contact, organization, technology, outdoor, science,

5

general culture, and arts and entertainment ("Career Counseling" by Elizabeth Yost and Anne Corbishley).

Many people choose an occupation they are familiar with. Possibly they follow in the footsteps of a parent, friend or relative. Some choose an occupation with money and prestige while others choose an occupation that helps others. Some people choose an occupation that has a promising future.

Just about every one choosing an occupation asks themselves the following questions:

- Am I good at it?

- Do I like it?

- What is the current job market like?

Guidance counselors have tests to answer the first two questions and are often aware of the job market. Vocational tests are even available on the internet. The "Kiersey Temperment Sorter" will classify you into Artisans, Guardians, Idealists or Rationals. "MyNextMove" uses the Department of Labor Holland Codes and will ask you about actual work tasks. Holland divided work environments into Realistic, Investigative, Artistic, Social, Enterprising, and Conventional.

The "Sokanu Career Test" will match you to a career based on your interests, personality, workplace, and history & goals. Loyola University of Chicago has a test to help you choose a major. The 123Test will help you choose a career based on the categories of investigative, social, conventional, real, artistic and enterprising. Do not take any of these tests too seriously. Loyal University thinks I should major in "environmental policy". I Have no idea what that is. Also, I have played and composed music my whole life and the 123Test put the "artistic" category next to last for me because music is the only art I favor.

Other considerations for choosing a career include:

- Is it physical or mental work?
- Do I sit at a desk or am I on my feet?
- Am I primarily indoors or outdoors?
- Will the job involve travel?
- Can I work in a small town?
- Do I work mostly alone or with others?
- Does the job involve creativity?
- Do I work with numbers?
- Does the job involve a lot of writing or do I work with my hands?
- What machinery do I work with including computers?
- What are the opportunities for advancement?

When comparing occupations you might rate them on status, money, autonomy, creativity, job security and authority/power. Obviously, some occupations require a considerable amount of education or training.

In my opinion, job location is underrated as to importance. Do you like a big city or a small town? A warm or cold climate? What recreational activities are nearby? Sports teams? Music? Restaurants? Many people wait until retirement to live where they really want to be.

All of the above are important considerations. Merit is the forgotten dimension. Some occupations let you rise to the top on well-defined merit. Success in other occupations depends on who you know, degrees and certificates, or appearances.

Let me give you two examples. Suppose you are a 16 year old right out of reform school who writes an app for Apple. Does Apple care about your age, education or character? Not if this app looks like something everyone will want. Being a professor in computer science gives you no advantage. All that counts is how many people want the app.

Now suppose you would like to be a commentator on Fox News. You are a woman who graduated at the top of the class in journalism. However, you are grossly overweight. Do you think you can rise to the top at Fox News on merit?

It has been said that one should write from one's own experience. The best way for me to demonstrate "The Forgotten Dimension" is to give you my story. My story is extreme as you shall soon see. By telling it I am hoping I might save some young person from making the same mistake I made.

Part I

I once attended a seminar where I was told that most people develop their view of the world when they are about ten years old. Accordingly, people who were ten during the great depression of the 1930's become very tight with money. People who were ten during World War II are often very patriotic. I was ten years old in the 1950's. My father was an engineer. My mother was an excellent piano player and a church organist. We loved watching "The Hit Parade" on television. My sister learned piano while I took up the trumpet. I wrote my first song while in junior high school. Even though I was young, I knew that songs like "You ain't nothing but a hound dog" and "My bucket has a hole in it" were only hits because of Elvis and Ricky Nelson. I loved composing but clearly songwriting was a career where you had to know the right people.

One of my best friends played trombone and another played the French horn. Unfortunately, there existed very little music for brass trio. Consequently, while in high school I embarked on writing considerable brass trio music for us to play. I also wrote a brass quartet that was performed at a school function. I even wrote a complete band number that was played at graduation. Isn't the cardinal rule that I should choose an occupation I really enjoyed?

I seriously considered majoring in music in college. My highest score on the Strong Inventory was "musician performer". The Strong Inventory is a test to determine the occupations with which you would feel the most comfortable. If you answer questions similar to an accountant, you would get a high score for accountant even if it is an occupation you never considered. Also, the Strong Inventory is not an ability test. You might feel comfortable in an occupation for which you have no talent. However, even with my limited knowledge of how musicians make a living I knew I had problems. For starters, I was not a wiz at playing the trumpet. I was not on the first stand in high school, never mind the first chair. Furthermore, playing solos made me nervous. On the other hand, I thought I knew what good music should sound like.

I must admit I did have an advantage composing music as I was able to play simple tunes on the trombone, clarinet, guitar, violin, piano, and drums. I was one of the first to have a reel to reel tape recorder in the 1960's that allowed me to do sound on sound so I could accompany myself on several instruments. My dream was to write music for the movies. As young and idealistic as I was, I knew that the chance of me becoming a screen composer was very small. I had no connections in Hollywood and had no idea how I would go about making some. Plus, I was a shy person. I was afraid that if I majored in music I would end up living above someone's garage.

A more serious problem for me with majoring in music is that I could not fall back on teaching. I am not a detail person. Later in life I taught statistics at a local university. I discovered that the last person who should teach math is someone who is good at it. I would not be good at explaining the steps of learning how to play the trumpet any more than I was good at explaining statistics. Furthermore, patience is not one of my virtues.

As it turned out, music became a strong hobby of mine producing very little money but lots of enjoyment.

(Check out "jalex1717" on YouTube for some of my music.) Consequently, when choosing an occupation, consider whether one of your choices would make a suitable hobby. You might enjoy golf but would you like spending eight hours a day at it as a professional?

Like so many college students I spent the first two years of college looking for a major. Like my father, who was an engineer, I was good at math. However, I am not a visual person, a trait that would be useful for an engineer. Plus I was more of a thinking person than a hands on person who liked to putter around. On the other hand, my brother had the visual ability. He made toy tanks and airplanes out of wood. He ended up with a degree in physics.

As it turned out, I enjoyed the social sciences – psychology, sociology and anthropology. Psychology appeared to have the best career choice in the social sciences. So I took as many psychology courses as possible. A career in psychology requires an advanced degree. I went on to get a Ph.D. from the University of Texas. I got accepted at the University of Texas in large part by scoring high on the Graduate Record Exam. I scored at the 88 percentile in verbal ability and at the 99 percentile in quantitative ability. In addition to the verbal and quantitative sections, you have the option to choose a subject matter test. Of course I choose the test in psychology. Evidently psychology was a good match for me as I scored two levels above the 99th percentile.

Ironically, when I was already working on my dissertation, Arnold Buss, a prominent psychologist, heard the University of Texas Jazz Band play one of my compositions. He told me I should have majored in music. A little late but thanks anyway.

Finding a job after graduation turned out to be easy. After turning down one job offer, I accepted a position at Brainerd State Hospital in Minnesota. This was primarily a hospital for the retarded but had recently opened up a psychiatric unit that served the mentally ill and the chemically dependent. The newness of this facility gave me the chance to provide input on its treatment programs. As a student I had worked one summer at St. Peter State Hospital and another summer at the St. Cloud VA hospital so I was very familiar with psychiatric patients. The psychiatrist at Brainerd State Hospital was very progressive. We had no locked doors during the daytime and every patient was assigned a counselor. We had a variety of activities for our patients including counseling, lectures, medications, occupational therapy, industrial assignments and family therapy. Unlike most psychiatric hospitals, those persons with advanced degrees did not call most of the shots. We had a counselor based program as these were the people who knew the patients the best. The psychiatrist, psychologist and social worker, set up programs and acted as consultants to the counselors. Nurses and psychiatric technicians also provided input to the counselors.

My father was a brilliant engineer but unfortunately he had an alcohol problem. He had been to Alcoholics Anonymous. He had seen a psychiatrist. Nothing seemed to work. His addiction lead to an early death at the age of 57 when I was still in college. Consequently, I decided to make the addictions one of my specialties. Our chemical dependency program followed those at other state hospitals at that time. It was based on AA and the counselors were former alcoholics.

Alcoholism is a major problem in northern Minnesota. The winters are brutal and northern Minnesota is not in the Bible belt. Taverns were a hub of activity in the surrounding small towns. We had a few patients at Brainerd State Hospital with other drug addictions but alcoholism was our primary concern. Logging and mining were big business in northern Minnesota in the early 1900's. The three largest employers in Brainerd when I was there in the 1970's was a lumber mill, the railroad, and our state hospital.

Being fresh out of college I did considerable research into the addictions. At the time, all of the state hospitals had programs based on Alcoholics Anonymous. Not surprisingly, the research literature had nothing to support the effectiveness or ineffectiveness of Alcoholics Anonymous. AA has a lot of testimonials including books by recovering alcoholics. They have clearly helped a lot of people. I am not criticizing AA. They have no money for research. However, I am questioning why taxpayers should support an AA based hospital program when AA is offered for free in most communities?

One thing was clear. About one-third of our admissions were readmissions. It made no sense to me to put them through the same 12 step AA based program. Plus our readmissions had a knack for saying all of the things that the staff liked to hear. They learned these phrases from their previous admissions.

Consequently, I worked on developing a second program for the chemically dependent. One that would be especially geared toward readmissions. This program was called "Time Structuring". An alcoholic spends considerable time around his addiction. Take away his addiction and how is he going to spend his time? AA meetings can only take you so far. These people need to develop meaningful and enjoyable interests that do not involve alcohol. Consequently, this idea would be the center of this new program.

"Time Structuring" also had a number of patients with mental illness as well as an addiction. Depressed people often turn to alcohol. Manic depressives are known to abuse alcohol. Even a schizophrenic might try alcohol as a medication.

I needed a counselor for this program. One with a natural ability that I lacked. Fortunately I found the perfect counselor for this program. He had a degree in recreation. Even better, he was a local resident with the usual interests in hunting and fishing. He was friendly and a good listener with a sense of humor.

Our program centered on each patient selecting activities they believed would keep their interest. We emphasized that some of these interests should involve family members or other people in the community. We did our best to place a time or number on these interests so that they were measurable. Whereas the AA program used weekend passes as a reward for good behavior, those in the Time Structuring program were to use weekend passes to try out new behaviors. It is all too easy for an alcoholic to feel his problems have been solved while in a controlled environment.

So how were we to know if our patients were following the program? Fortunately, we were able to obtain two Volunteers in Service to America (VISTA). It was their job to visit our patients at their homes. They could work with our patients and former patients to help achieve the goals created at the hospital. They could talk to family and friends to see if our discharged patients were following through with their plans developed at the hospital.

The Time Structuring program had some other differences from the traditional AA program. For example, in addition to informal talking, we engaged our patients in role playing. It has been my experience that alcoholics talk a great game but often act in a contrary manner. Role playing highlights situations that the person is not yet able to handle in the best possible way. For example, we might role play a person being offered a drink by someone who insists that one drink won't hurt them. We might also role play meeting a new neighbor. Role playing allows other members of the group to offer suggestions. This can give the counselor a pass from being "the authority." Reversing roles can be highly informative. The counselor can play the patient and the patient can play the counselor or perhaps the patient could play his or her own spouse. It is always interesting to see what advice a patient gives himself. Many a big talker failed miserably at role playing. We believed that the ability to understand and respond appropriately to a variety of situations was a good predictor of success in the community.

Probably our most innovative idea was "Nightclubbing". We actually took a small number of patients to a local bar with a counselor and VISTA person.

There the patient would learn to order a nonalcoholic beverage, engage in conversation, play pool or hit the dance floor. This activity involves the standard psychological techniques called "desensitization" and "exposure and response stopping". Our patients learned to feel comfortable ordering nonalcoholic drinks. One of our patients commented on how he would ask a lady to dance while the regulars were having a few drinks to build up courage. Unfortunately we had too small of a sample to do a research project on this activity. In any case, I expect most treatment centers would not try this activity for fear of lawsuits. Plus, they would need high level staff to work nights.

The bottom line is that the Time Structuring program received an award from the National Institute of Drug Abuse for its innovation.

In addition to chemical dependency, my other specialty I developed is called program evaluation. Anyone can create a treatment program. How do we know if it is any good? Feedback is the only way to make improvements. The state of Minnesota spends a lot of money to house and treat the mentally ill and chemically dependent. How does the taxpayer know if the money is well spent?

Through my efforts I convinced the staff to use the Personal Adjustment and Role Skills (PARS) inventory for every admission to Brainerd State Hospital. This questionnaire is sent to a patient's significant other. This person could be a spouse, relative, friend or employer. The PARS covers a wide variety of behaviors from symptoms of anxiety, depression and drug/alcohol abuse to marital status and employment. This same inventory was repeated one month and six months after discharge. Furthermore, upon leaving the hospital, we asked our patients to rank our various treatments and activities as to how helpful they were. We also kept track of readmissions.

I helped create a patient goals checklist to further help evaluate the improvement of our patients. The checklist listed eleven areas such as communications, interpersonal relationships, self-care, mood, and addictions. An example of a communications goal would be "needs to make his or her wants clear." An example of a mood goal would be "needs to be less anxious."

As chairman of the Minnesota Psychologists in State Service, I instituted the first follow-up study where pairs of psychologists rated incoming patients and later repeated these ratings at the person's home. This study was done for psychiatric patients from all of the state hospitals in Minnesota. In large part because of our ongoing effort to evaluate our services, Brainerd State Hospital became one of only seven multi-service hospitals (i.e., those that treat the mentally ill, the chemically dependent and the retarded) in the United States to be fully accredited.

I also wrote an evaluation plan for a proposed corrections program called Probation Offenders Rehabilitation Training (PORT). Brainerd was selected as one of three areas in the state of Minnesota. I helped PORT in the selection of persons who could enter this program. This program had no locks and bars so we needed to be selective in who we chose. My favorite interview question was "what animal would you like to be?" I was wary of the staying power of anyone who wanted to be a bird.

I also taught law enforcement people in northern Minnesota how to deal with the mentally ill. Fifty years later, many policemen still do not know how to handle someone who is mentally ill. For example. I suggested a law officer ask for the person's name before bellowing out instructions like "get down". A schizophrenic or a person high on drugs will know their name. They might get shot "resisting arrest" before they figure out that "get down" means to get on the ground.

Given my experience, I created and chaired a two day conference on program evaluation with speakers and attendees from all over the state of Minnesota. At the time I believed that we needed a way to measure the milieu of our state hospitals. I thought that a hospital environment that was supportive and caring might be as effective as any specific treatments given. I was influenced by a tour I took of one of our local prisons. Is it possible that seeing bars every day and being ordered around convinces an inmate that he is indeed a bad person and incapable of managing his own life?

The above is a summary of my five years as a psychologist. I thought it was a successful and productive time for me. My wife at this time was from San Antonio. As previously mentioned, I received my Ph.D. from the University of Texas at Austin. Texas might be hot but it was still better than the bitter cold of Minnesota. Any winter day when the temperature rose above zero was considered a good day. I had gotten a job offer in Santa Fe, New Mexico but it fell through when a person decided to transfer from Albuquerque. We decided to move back to Texas. Of course it is not a good idea to move without a job but it is hard to get a job without a personal interview. Plus, I thought I had a solid resume.

I know it took a while but we are getting to the part about the forgotten dimension for choosing an occupation. After working for five years as a psychologist in Minnesota, I spent five years applying for jobs in Texas. I applied for jobs in Dallas, Houston, and San Antonio but mostly in Austin. Austin being the capitol of Texas had the administrative jobs that suited me. One position I applied for involved evaluating the state hospitals in Texas. Surprisingly, I was not a shoe-in for this position although I did make the second interview. Another job involved setting up community programs for the chemically dependent. Again I made that second interview. Furthermore, I was in contact with a person from Fort Worth who was interested in evaluating a variety of services. The only feedback I received from applying for a job was that "I claimed too much on my resume."

I know why I was passed over for several counseling positions. When they asked what tests I administered I replied "I am not aware of any psychological tests that help people get better." I was a true behaviorist. I believed in interviews and observations. People who brought someone to our state hospital expected us to test this person and report back with a label such as depression or schizophrenia. I insisted that they tell us what this person does that makes them think that he or she belongs in our hospital. This is known as "a ticket of admission". Hearing voices that no one else hears is a ticket. Never leaving the house is a ticket. Suicidal puts you at the front of the line.

I am a believer in a comprehensive interview with the patient as well as interviews with any significant others in his or her life. Interviews get to the real behaviors that are of concern to others. Psychiatric hospitals are known for working on a person's schizophrenia when the family is more concerned with inappropriate social behaviors such as talking to uninterested strangers.

As it was, we gave all of our admissions to Brainerd State Hospital the Minnesota Multiphasic Personality Inventory (MMPI). Not only was I very familiar with this test, I had spoken to one of its creators. Fortunately, I did not have to create a profile from their answers and write an interpretation. Even in the mid 1970's there was a pharmaceutical company that did this by computer for a fee. To be truthful, our staff loved reading these patient descriptions. They made our medical records look very professional. Unfortunately, I cannot remember this test leading to any great insights on how we should treat our patients. However, this test is useful if you want to label patients, something insurance companies require.

In all fairness, I am all for tests that help people make decisions. I would have loved to have had a test that indicated which persons would likely benefit from psychotropic medications. Knowing that a person is schizophrenic is not enough. Many diagnosed schizophrenics do not respond to medication. As a behaviorist I could endorse many tests of depression. They ask questions such as "Do you have trouble sleeping?" "Have your eating habits changed?" "Have you lost your desire for sex?" These same types of behavioral questions can be used to assess change.

Recently I contacted the Licensing Boards for counselors in several states. I suggested that pre and post testing should be a requirement for maintaining a counseling license. Here is what I wrote the Board of Psychologists for the state of Virginia:

Dear Members of the Board:

Virginia has some of the strictest standards for licensing counseling psychologists. However, I believe they are not strict enough. Although Virginia psychologists are well trained, they can only get better with feedback from clients and family members. I am proposing the following conditions for licensing:

(1) All licensed counselors are to do pre and post testing using a standardized instrument.

(2) The preferred instrument is the current Diagnostic and Statistical Manual of Mental Disorders (DSM-5) that has symptom measures that consists of 23 questions in 13 diagnostic categories. If a client scores high on a diagnostic category such as depression, he or she is asked additional questions in that category (8 questions for depression).

(3) Answers to these symptom checklists would go to a centralized database as well as to the counselor.

(4) Pre-testing would be within the first three sessions of counseling. Post-testing would occur upon discharge and six months after treatment.

(5) Also upon discharge the client/patient would fill out a standardized form that goes directly to the state regarding his or her perception of the treatment process and the skills of the counselor. This form would to be devised by a committee.

(6) Procedures would be taken so that clients/patients in the database are not identifiable.
(7) Each counselor would receive a yearly summary of these results.

Obviously, the above checklists cannot be done on every client/patient for a variety of reasons that a counselor could indicate on an exception form.

In the state of Virginia <u>not a single counselor</u> supported my idea. I have spoken to many counselors and I have yet to meet one that routinely does pre and post testing. Evidently, they rely on the patient for verbal feedback who cannot be trusted to be completely honest. In college, I studied something called "cognitive dissonance". It predicts that a person's beliefs will line up with one's behavior. In other words, if you spent six months in therapy and claimed no improvement, you would not only be crazy but stupid.

I spoke before the licensing board for the state of Texas. I knew that pre and post testing was too much to expect, so I tried to convince them to set up a web site where individuals who received counseling could give feedback. Presently, there are websites that rate physicians but the questions asked such as "how long did you have to wait to see the doctor" and "how did the staff treat you" are not relevant for counselors.

I created my own list of questions for people who had been in counseling as follows (See Appendix 1 for the complete list):

1. Was your counselor a good listener?
2. Did your counselor assign homework?

3. Did your counselor ask to speak with someone that knows you?

The bottom line is that with all of my training and experience, there is no way for me to recommend a good therapist if you are looking for one. If you were to ask an advice columnist how to choose a therapist, she would probably recommend someone who is licensed by the state. To be licensed by the state you must have a minimum of a master's degree and pass a national counselor exam. Would you believe the exam is multiple choice? Knowing about counseling and being a good counselor are two different things. Writing a book on counseling does not make you a good counselor any more than writing a screenplay makes you a good actor.

So who are the best counselors, social workers, psychologists or psychiatrists? As it turns out, I am one of the few people who knows who make the best counselors. It is all in my book - *Counseling: A profession or a trade?* (An e-book at Amazon). Paraprofessionals make the best counselors; that is, persons with less than a master's degree. This research was done in the 1980's. Very little research has been done since when it became obvious that nobody cares. Of course that means that the best counselors cannot be licensed.

Given I sold few copies of my book, I created a summary that I sent to various magazines to no avail (see Appendix 2). *Scientific American Mind* had a section called myths in psychology. Evidently they thought the idea that counselors need a master's degree and certification to be effective was no myth. I had no better luck with the sections on health in various popular magazines. I also turned my views on counseling into a potential Ted Talk to no avail (See Appendix 3).

I believe the best counselors are naturals. These are people who grew up listening to the problems of others and settling disputes. These are people who are empathetic and nonjudgmental. I have 96 semester hours in psychology. I have never seen a class called "Developing Empathy". If people could be taught to be nonjudgmental I would be giving out gift certificates at Christmas. I do not know of any graduate school in counseling refusing admission to an 'A' student because he was more of a talker than a listener. Fortunately, if you are a natural counselor you can become a life coach. It is only a matter of time before some graduate student compares licensed counselors to life coaches. Don't bet on the counselor.

During the five years I spent looking for work as a psychologist, I did have some interesting learning experiences. I was the "gringo" in two different Tex-Mex bands. One of these bands was in Austin, Texas. Austin is the music capitol of the southwest and our bandleader said you can always get a job in other parts of Texas by being from Austin. This band was unusual for me as they had no sheet music to read. I had to listen to recordings and then wing it. I will never forget that when I told the band members that I was moving to San Antonio, a couple of the band members cried! Unless I join another Hispanic band, that was sure to be a once in a lifetime experience.

During the day I worked for Manpower. I would show up at their office every morning and most of the time they had work for me to do. I unloaded trucks and trains, did warehouse work and various cleaning. My first discovery is that some men liked the freedom of day to day work. To my surprise, one of these day laborers had rental property. I found it ironic that one of my jobs involved sweeping the floor of a local book store used by the students at the University of Texas. I figured if I saw anyone looking over the psychology books, I was sure they would like some tips from the cleaning man.

I spent a couple of weeks as the dishwasher at an insurance company. There I learned the meaning of patronizing. Most people ignored me when they returned their dirty dishes. The few who spoke with me always smiled and spoke slowly and clearly so I would understand them.

I eventually got a job on a short term research project studying tri-ethnic segregation; that is the distribution of whites, blacks and Hispanics. I was able to use my knowledge of statistics and programming to create a measure of tri-ethnic segregation of housing. I learned that over time, racial integration is <u>not</u> happening. It only appears that way as the population grows because the transition areas between blacks and whites look like areas of integration (See Appendix 4).

My wife and I eventually moved to San Antonio where we could live with her grandparents in an old 30 by 40 foot wooden house close to the downtown. Her grandfather worked every day in the back yard creating concrete benches, tables, flower pots, and statues from molds. To him, every day was the same. He had no conception of a day of rest. I did his taxes for him. Even though he often dealt with cash, he kept good records of his sales and listed every penny on his taxes. He was probably the most honest man I would ever meet.

While in San Antonio I worked on construction building a gas station. I was a gymnast at the University of Minnesota and I thought I was in good shape to work construction. That is, until I tried using a jackhammer, a 90 pound weapon that jerks you around like a rag doll.

I also played in a band that played half old standards and half salsa music. To me, salsa music is the most danceable music in the world. This band had two percussionists from Cuba who played the timbales and many other percussion instruments I cannot name. We played a lot of weddings that included free food. Weddings in San Antonio often had our band plus a mariachi group. This was the peak of my trumpet skills as I played on a regular basis.

While in San Antonio I worked on a book called "Mind Skills". Finally I could do something in psychology again. I based this book on some classes I had for patients and staff at Brainerd State Hospital. This was a considerable work with 15 chapters. These chapters included Relaxation Training, Achieving Goals, Breaking Habits, Creative Problem Solving, Improving your Memory, Decision Making, Getting Along with Others, Illness and Health, and Mental Disorders.

In this book I had my own theory of dream interpretation that I call "levels of dreaming" (Appendix 5). The lowest level of dreaming involves housekeeping – categorizing, consolidating and discarding. Indeed, even today many neurologists think that is all that dreaming does and therefore dream interpretation is a waste of time. I can guarantee you that these people have never had a lucid dream when you are "awake" in a dream.

In my book I also discuss the basic operating principles of the mind with no references to neurology. Surprisingly, some thirty years later there has been a revival of books on brain power, mostly by learned scholars. I got as far as a publisher deciding between my manuscript and someone else's. I lost!

I also spent some time in Colorado Springs where I taught a class on alcoholism and did a few seminars on "Mind Skills" for private companies. I loved the very changeable weather in Colorado Springs. I remember 3 feet of snow in winter that shut everything down, and a day in February when the temperature hit 70 degrees.

While in Colorado Springs my wife and I also worked on a cognitive therapy we called "semantic readjustment". The crux of this therapy was to look at a person's problems and analyze them as if it were a dream. For example, if you were fired from a job you could not blame your boss or the economy. This is a dream. Everything was created by you out of your desires and belief systems. Possibly there was a good reason for this unpleasant experience. Perhaps at a deeper level you did not feel you deserved this job. The power of this approach is that it only deals with what you have control over – yourself.

By now you are probably thinking that this book is sour grapes. I had unusual experiences job hunting and have created a theory to explain my plight. Please hold your judgment until you have read part two.

Part II

With no job available in mental health, I eventually, I got a full time job at a regional education service center evaluating school programs. Mathematics and statistics was my minor in college and I was able to use these skills to evaluate various education programs. One of the more unusual programs I evaluated was school bus driver training. In order to evaluate the training I had to become a certified school bus driver. Now if I am ever broke again I know where I can get a job.

I supplemented my income by teaching "Statistics for Business" at the University of Texas at San Antonio. There were two other teachers for this subject but my class quickly filled up as the other teachers did not speak good English. I supplemented the textbook with real examples from my regular job. I discovered that even my best students were bewildered when I gave them a problem that included data that was not relevant to the solution. The students thought I was trying to "trick" them when I was only demonstrating the problem with textbook examples.

The head of the math department called me in one day and told me that the grades I was giving were too high. I offered a simple solution to his problem. Since there were three of us teaching the same subject, we could all use the same tests and someone other than myself could assign grades. That was the last I heard from him.

My job evaluating education programs required government funding which soon ran low. I applied for a temporary job at Fort Sam Houston automating the tracking of 18,000 medical personnel in the military. This was in the 1980's when people began to use personal computers.

I became a one-man data processing department. I turned on the mainframe in the morning and took the saves in the afternoon. I wrote a menu driven system for entering and checking data. The computer kept track of all of the data changes and who made them. I created several menu driven reports. I even created a way to get to the source data from a menu for each major computer module. When I was finished two years later I received an award (no money) for saving 500 man-hours per month. I essentially did the work of a consultant as a federal GS-9 (mid-level).

From there I got another government job tracking the flow of traffic on the rivers and waterways. At this job we switched all of our computer programs over from COBOL to 'C' and Oracle. I became the database administrator. Oracle was fairly new software. Because I worked with it on a day to day basis, I had Oracle consultants ask me questions. I attended Oracle's ten year convention where I was told that Oracle had doubled it worth every year for ten years! Too bad I had not bought their stock.

I eventually moved up to become the manager of Data Processing. I had seven people under me including two people with master's degrees in computer science. At one time we were told we had to use a computer language called "Ada" but I refused. Later that order was rescinded.

I know it was a long time coming but this is the interesting part. I have 96 semester credit hours in psychology and five years of experience and could not get a job as a psychologist. I have zero credits in computer science and ended up running a small data processing office. How is that possible?

The answer is <u>the merit scale</u>. What is the merit scale? The merit scale measures how important merit is regarding your success. Are you selected for a job according to merit? Are you paid according to merit? Do you rise up in your company according to merit? Let's assume the merit scale ranges from zero to ten. Zero means that merit is completely unrelated to success whereas ten means that merit is the only thing that counts. Let us look at some different occupations.

Counseling Psychologists

Let us rate the occupation of counseling on the merit scale. Suppose we have a city with 100 counselors and were are able to accurately rank them on merit/ability. Perhaps the best we have is the ratings from one to ten by former clients. Let us assume that the best counselor has an average rating of 9.0 and the worst counselor has a rating of 3.0. How much more per hour does the best counselor charge? Unless the best counselor has a radio or television program or a bestselling book, chances are he or she charges about the same as the worst counselor.

Counselors with Ph.D.'s probably charge somewhat more than counselors with a master's degree. Is there any evidence that Ph.D.'s make better counselors? None that I know of. Counselors with a specialty such as family counseling, anger management, or substance abuse might

30

charge somewhat more. Credentials do not count in the merit system unless there is concrete evidence that they are related to merit. At this point in time, we do not know if Ph.D.'s with specialties are better counselors than life coaches with high school educations.

Are Ph.D.'s with additional certification in substance abuse better counselors than recovering alcoholics or addicts? We do not know the answer because so few treatment centers do the follow up on how many of their clients have been sober/clean for one year. As I mentioned earlier, my counselor for the "Time Structuring" program had a degree in recreation. Our three other counselors for the chemically dependent were recovering alcoholics. The hospital where I worked also had three counselors for the mentally ill, all with bachelor degrees. One of these counselors had a major in the theater. Another one of these counselors went out of her way to learn how to apply behavioral principles to her patients.

The good news is that many individual counselors work with depressed clients. There exist several measures of depression that makes it be easy to do before and after treatment measurements. In fact the new Diagnostic Statistical Manuel (DSM-5) consists of questions in several different areas that can be used for before and after ratings. Unfortunately, if the counselor does both before and after ratings, we might consider those ratings to be biased. It would be better to have the client or a significant other do pre and post ratings. Ideally there would be at least two post ratings - one at the completion of counseling and one several months later.

As I mentioned earlier, you need to pass a multiple choice national exam to become a licensed counselor. Is there any evidence that persons who score high on this exam make better counselors than people who barely pass? This would be a good dissertation for some graduate student. Unfortunately, we cannot compare high scorers with people who fail the exam. I like to tell people that I could be playing my trumpet with a major symphony orchestra if all I needed was to pass a multiple choice exam in music. I believe that licensing counselors should at least involve judging an actual session of counseling. If the judges cannot agree with each other, we have a more serious issue regarding counseling.

To be a counselor you need a master's degree. How many 'A' students who are talkers go into counseling to appear wise? How many counselors who are taught that giving advice is not counseling, give advice anyway? Every counselor needs to give out some information. She might even talk about what usually works for someone with a similar problem. The problem with giving advice is that it shifts the responsibility of getting better from the client to the counselor. Good advice teaches the client to go to someone for advice when in trouble. Bad advice can sabotage the entire counseling process. Dr. Phil has a great show but it is not an example of counseling. No one wants to hear Dr. Phil spend an hour saying "How did that make you feel? Tell me more." Furthermore, confrontation is not a commonly used technique in counseling. A good counselor facilitates the client to discover his own solution.

If you know a counselor, ask her the following questions:

1. Who is harder to treat? A person with anxiety and depression or a person who is an addicted to drugs or alcohol? The overwhelming majority of counselors will say a person who is addicted to drugs or alcohol is more difficult to treat. Then ask the next question.
2. Why do you need the minimum of a master's degree to treat anxiety and depression when a recovering addict with two years of college can treat another addict? Perhaps if you have recovered from depression, you should be able to treat a depressed person with two years of training.

I have an entire e-book available from Amazon titled "Counseling: A Profession or a Trade" devoted to arguing that counseling should be a trade. It is backed up by studies by Ph.D. psychologists.

Skill training can be a valuable part of counseling or taught independently. People skills involve conflict resolution, active listening, and assertive training. I taught active listening to patients. Skills can be measured. With follow-up it can be ascertained if those skills make a difference. I also taught relaxation. There is evidence that meditation is a valuable skill for reducing anxiety. Today we have "mindfulness" which has a more Western flavor than meditation.

The bottom line is that I would give **counseling a score of 2** on the merit scale. Rising to the top depends on certificates, seminars (taught or taken) and salesmanship.

Evidence from pre and post testing is not relevant. I have applied for several psychologist positions and have **never** been asked if I had any evidence that I could improve someone's life. In other words, I am probably being generous in giving a score as high as a 2. In theory, counseling could have a score of zero. Why? Because the poorest counselors probably make the most money. Think about it. If the patients never get better they stay with the counselor until they cry "uncle" or until their money runs out.

Computer Programmers

Now let's look at the occupation of computer science. First of all, there is no such thing as computer "science" unless learning to type is typewriter science. What is called computer science is primarily a collection of languages. If it were a science, people would observe computers and come up with hypotheses such as "A watched computer never sorts" and "No matter how long you wait to buy a computer, you will wish you had waited longer".

So how important is a degree in data processing to rise to the top? Bill Gates did pretty well without a college degree and so did Mark Zuckerberg. I wonder how rich Bill Gates would be if he had developed an improved method of counseling?

It is difficult to measure the effects of counseling. People seek counseling at a low point so that most would improve on their own. People will tell you they are better and even believe it themselves when there is no solid evidence of improvement. Most research projects use a control group that does not receive counseling. Not all control groups are equal. Sham therapy is a better control group than delayed therapy.

Computer programs either work as they are supposed to or they don't. If you downloaded an app to find the closest restaurant and was sent to a gas station, you would know that the app was flawed.

A program that runs as expected does not necessarily rate an 'A'. Programs need to be well documented and elegant. Elegant usually means written in the simplest way to achieve the desired results. Convoluted programs are referred to as "spaghetti". People who write spaghetti programs either get fired or have a job for life. New programmers who have to modify someone else's code have been known to rewrite code from scratch. It is possible to be self-taught and write elegant code although a computer class would not hurt anyone. Many computer languages, such as Java, are modular. A module does a specific task and can be used in several different programs.

I would give the **occupation of programmer a 9** on the merit scale. Note that computer science includes specialties such as network communications, database administrator, systems analyst and web designer. In any case, if you can make things work in data processing and keep them working you can probably get by with tattoos and an anti-social personality in this occupation. Furthermore, you can make a small fortune by selling an app that makes life easier or by creating an interesting game.

Had I known about merit in college, I could have saved myself four years' worth of psychology courses. I should mention that I worked as a psychologist before they had licensing. If I were a licensed psychologist and kept it up, I could have worked as an independent counselor and I would have had a job for life. To be licensed in the state of Louisiana, I would have to start graduate school all over. The State of Louisiana allows me no credit for my five years of work as a psychologist.

Physicians

A psychologist can lose his license by seducing a patient or outright fraud, but the likelihood of losing your license as the result of incompetence is next to nothing. Without pre and post data, how would you know if a psychologist was incompetent? A physician can actually lose his or her license for incompetence. That is one reason I have to rate physicians slightly higher on the merit scale - <u>probably a 4</u>. I cannot rate them any higher because an exceptional family doctor probably makes less money than an incompetent specialist. Furthermore, insurance providers, including Medicare, make it difficult for better doctors to make more money (although they can try to charge more).

People often ask friends for a recommendation on who is a good physician. It has been my experience that people recommend a physician who

- Does not have a long wait time regarding both the day and the time.

- Is a good listener.

- Treats you like an equal.

These are mostly the characteristics of a good person, although you would also want a physician with these qualities. As to your doctor's medical skill, how would you know if your physician is better than others? You might if he or she clearly misdiagnosed you. How would you know if the drugs your doctor prescribes are the recommendations of a drug rep or from reading a respected journal? Pharmaceutical salesmen are often attractive young ladies who come with lunch or other gifts. That should make you uncomfortable that the medicine you are prescribed is truly safe and effective.

In my opinion, the future of medicine will even lower physicians on the merit scale. I see computers taking over many of their duties. Chess masters are some of the brightest people in the world but even the best are no match for a computer. Computers will soon become the primary source for diagnosis. Television shows about doctors once demonstrated how the best of doctors or interns could properly diagnose a patient. A doctor with years of experience will be no match for a computer with over a million cases. DXplain helped a Seattle doctor diagnose an illness that occurs in 1 in 4,000 people as well as led to dramatic savings at the Mayo Clinic (Scientific American, August 2017, p.24-25). VisualDx improved the correct diagnosis of a skin infection by 50% (ibed). In the near future a computer will

(1) Consider a person's symptoms, medical history including medical procedures and medications, family history, lab tests, and eventually genome to come up with several diagnoses according to their probabilities of being accurate.

(2) Recommend further testing or observation if necessary.
(3) Prescribe medications. A computer will definitely be needed once a person's genome is in the computer. No doctor will be able to remember which medicines are best for which genomes.
(4) Tell you a physician is running 40 minutes late so you can minimize office wait time.

Genomes will revolutionize medicine. No longer will you have to search the world for a specialist to help you with an unknown disease or travel to Boston or the Mayo Clinic. The genome on a new born with convulsions led to an anti-seizure drug that was rarely uses on infants (*Time*, October 2017). Approximately 2000 diseases can be detected with genetic testing.

Your medical information needs to be stored in a uniform nationwide medical record. The United States military has one. How much time is wasted each year filling out medical forms for new physicians? This medical record should begin with patient comments. For example, I know of a person who was misdiagnosed as having Parkinson's disease. You can never get rid of a diagnosis but you can at least point this out in patient comments.

At the very least, in the future you should enter your doctor's office with your computer printout of what the computer suggests. This should save considerable time. I read an article in 2015 that predicted a physician shortage of 90,000 physicians in the near future. Given that the United States has about 970,000 physicians, a computer only needs to reduce a physician's workload by

10% to solve that crisis. Another solution to the physician shortage is to increase the number of nurse practitioners and physician assistants. No one coming for a checkup without symptoms needs to see a physician.

Surgeons

Surgeons are in a special category when it comes to the merit system. On the plus side, it is a bit easier to evaluate a successful surgery versus drug therapy. If they are a heart surgeon they might even have a mortality rating. Of course it may have been the anesthesiologist who killed the patient.

The problem I have with ratings surgeons is <u>that the best potential surgeons never get into medical school</u>. Surgery needs to be its own profession. What are some of the qualities of a good surgeon?

(1) Good hand to eye coordination.
(2) Fine motor skills
(3) Stamina for long operations
(4) Emotionally unflappable

How many of these qualities are measured on the MCAT? This is the test that gets you into medical school. None of these qualities are measured. The difference between being a regular physician and a surgeon is like the difference between a sports announcer and a player. The sports announcer may know more about football than the player but that does not qualify him to play the game. In fact, a study of 33 laparoscopic surgeons discovered that the number one predictor of surgical skills was how good they were at video games. Video game skills were ahead of years of training or number of surgeries performed in predictive power (*Scientific American Mind*, Jan/Feb 2013, P.34). I am guessing that your 'A' students in high school are not your best video game players.

I am about to say something that is sure to be controversial – You can improve the quality of medical care by paying physicians less money. Paying physicians less money will increase the number of women doctors. In the United States female primary care physicians average $192,000 per year compared to their male counterparts who average $225,000 (There are many internet sources on the wage differences between male and female physicians). I believe one reason that women will accept less money is that they see their job as a helping profession. In the United States, 34% of the physicians are women. In Finland, 56% of the physicians are women and in Russia the percent is 70%. The pay scale for physicians varies considerable by country. In Finland the salaries of a physician are only about twice that of teachers (who usually have a master's degrees). That probably explains why most of the physicians in Finland are women. Also, more primary grade teachers in Finland are men than the United States (21% vs 13%). You can also improve the quality of care by creating more nurse practitioners. In a 2013 study in the *Journal for Nurse Practitioners*, patients gave nurse practitioners 9.8 out of 10 in satisfaction whereas physicians only averaged 7.2.

Another reason why lower salaries will improve medical care is that it would increase the number of physicians that come here from foreign countries. A recent study (*BMJ* 2017; 356) found that interns who came here from foreign countries had a lower mortality rate among their patients than our native born physicians.

One reason why physicians' charges are high is because most physicians leave medical school with a lot of debt. The average medical students graduates with a debt about $170,000. The solution to this problem is for the government to pay this debt. In return, the physician would treat one of every ten patients (10%) for free. Of course these patients would have to be below the poverty level.

How does this work out over thirty years of practice? Let's suppose that physicians make $200,000 per year. Consequently, the people whose medical school was paid for would make only $180,000 per year because they treat 10% of their patients for free. With no debt these physicians could put aside 10% of their salaries ($18,000) and began making 5% simple interest once a year (mutual funds?). The physicians in debt would begin by putting aside 10% ($20,000) of their salaries to pay off their $170,000 of debt including 5% simple interest beginning with their first year of practice. They can pay off their debt in 7 years. For the next 23 years they can make 5% on $20,000 per year investments. How much will each of these physicians make over the course of 30 years? If you are not familiar with accumulating interest, the answer might surprise you. Before taxes the physicians who had no debt would make about $6,115,694 over 30 years. The physicians who had to first pay off their debt would make about $6,270,040 over 30 years. Is this not a reasonable deal for a physician and a great deal for the government? Of course these figures can change by manipulating the percentages but I am erring on the conservative side by assuming debtors pay the same interest on the dollar that investors make.

Automobile Mechanic

Car trouble is annoying. Finding a good mechanic is a joy. I had an independent mechanic for several years. He clearly explained what needed to be done. He let me know how serious a problem was and the cost of repairs. Sometimes I had the choice of using rebuilt parts or new ones. Looking back, I know nothing about his background or training. For all I know he could have been a self-taught high school dropout. I also have a nephew in another state who works on Mercedes. The dealership has sent him to more workshops for training and certification than I can count.

Why don't colleges include more internships before giving you a degree? If you are studying to be an engineer, shouldn't you intern with an engineering firm as a degree requirement? Shouldn't the same hold true for accountants, lawyers, MBA's, chemists, political science majors, etc.? Fortunately, many professions do require on the job experience. Education majors must do practice teaching. Architects must complete an internship. Music majors give recitals. Of course any form of on-the-job training gives you an income plus experience.

Going back to auto mechanic, the fact that I never asked for his "credentials" tells me right away that this is a job high on the merit scale. An ailing automobile differs from an ailing person in one very important aspect – most people will eventually get well on their own. No matter how long you leave your car in the garage, it is not going to improve on its own. Fixing cars relies on merit because people usually know when a car is fixed.

Of course some problems are more obvious than others. You can see with your own eyes that your tire is flat. You can see the steam from an over-heated radiator. You can hear a bad muffler. Other problems are more subtle. A friend had a car that periodically would not start. A dealer replaced the starter and solenoid but that did not fix the problem. Unfortunately, a low level mechanic does not understand systems. They keep replacing parts with the hope that one of these parts will do the trick.

Fixing an automobile can be expensive but it is easier to shop around for a mechanic than a physician. Also, in my opinion, a good referral is more reliable for an auto mechanic than for a physician. If you think fixing an automobile is expensive, what if they required a muffler specialist to first learn something about brakes, air-conditioning, transmissions, an internal combustion engines. Remember, your physician who performs your colonoscopy has to know something about your nose, ears and throat before specializing.

On the negative side, there are shady mechanics that will claim you need serious work when they know the problem is simple. This has been verified on a television show when they brought an automobile to various mechanics that simply had a disconnected wire. The guy who said "no charge" for fixing the problem probably got more business than he could handle. I give **auto mechanic a 7** on the merit scale.

Certified Public Accountant (CPA)

The qualifications to be a certified public account vary by state. However, most states require 150 hours of college including at least 24 semester hours in business/accounting. Nearly all states require a bachelor's degree. Fifteen years or more of public accounting experience approved by the State Board for Public Accountancy may be acceptable in place of formal education in New York. Some states require a year's experience as well as a bachelor's degree before taking the CPA exams. In Oregon "in order to be eligible for a CPA license, candidates must complete 12 months of qualifying experience under the direct supervision of a qualified supervisor."

So what is the CPA exam like? According to *topaccountingdegrees.org*, "The exam to become a CPA lasts a total of 14 hours, divided into four separate content sections: Auditing and Attestation (AUD), Business Environment and Concepts (BEC), Financial Accounting and Reporting (FAR), and Regulation (REG). Candidates must pass each section with a score of at least 75 on a scale of 0-99 to become certified as a public accountant." The exam consists of multiple choice question, writing, and case studies. Most candidates spend 300 to 400 hours studying for the exams. Even with all of that preparation, only about half of the applicants pass the exams.

Clearly, becoming a certified public accountant shows you are well qualified to do the job. So why do I only give **CPA a 7** on the merit scale? I give the job a 7 because with such a rigorous exam, I see no need to require all of those college credits. Let me explain.

While working with the federal government, I was involved with the hiring of a lot of people for the position of statistician. Math was my minor in college. I taught a few classes of "Statistics for Business" at the University of

Texas at San Antonio. To insure that our applicants knew basic statistics, I created a true or false test from introductory statistics. Unfortunately, the government did not allow me to use this test of basic statistical knowledge for people applying to be statisticians. My hope was that people who had passed a class in statistics years ago had retained this knowledge. Given the choice between old transcripts and current testing, I would choose current testing every time. I wonder if anyone has even done the correlation between CPA exam scores and previous grades. Of course if there were a high correlation there would be no need for the exams.

However, my main reason for excluding college grades is that the need to attend college to get an education is so 1980's. Young people communicate with each other by texting and colleges still think they need to hear a personal lecture to learn. For most subjects, learning over the internet or by DVD is not only better than a traditional lecture but immensely cheaper.

The following is a comparison of a classroom lecture versus instruction via the Internet or DVD.

	Classroom	Computer
Teacher:	Average	Exceptional
Visual Aids:	Minimal	Extensive
Repeating:	Embarrassing	Trivial
Getting there:	Driving, walking	As close as your computer
Questions:	Teacher	Chat group

The cost of learning via computer is a great savings over a classroom. For example, I can download 36 half-hour lectures of Calculus II from a well-known internet company for $319.95; on sale for $74.95. I can download 60 half-hour chemistry lectures for $529.95; on sale for $149.95. Although this internet company does not have a DVD called "Accounting", they do have 25 courses in the fields of economics and finance. A college in Columbia, Missouri does have an on-line accounting program. The Massachusetts Institute of Technology offers free accounting courses through its OpenCourseWare (OCW) systems.

One of the principle advantages of computer learning is that you can go at your own pace. Some people may want to rerun several lessons while others race ahead. A good learning program tests your comprehension as you go along to keep you at a pace that suits you. A classroom teacher has to deal with students who very widely in their ability to comprehend the lessons. An exceptionally bright student might enter college at age 14. However, once in college she can only progress ahead of the others by taking more credits. This means she must work on a variety of subject matter instead of focusing on a limited number of areas.

Teachers

Given so many occupations require college credits, let us consider the occupation of teacher. Evaluating teachers has always been a touchy subject. Usually the principal does the evaluations for grade school teachers. Many colleges let students grade the teachers. Evaluating middle and high school teachers creates the most controversy. The most popular evaluation approach is to follow the test scores of their pupils. I am talking about standardized tests with nationwide norms. Although a teacher cannot be responsible for any one child, the average success of their pupils over the course of several years should indicate something about their ability to teach.

You can compare the improvement of students from an earlier test to a later one. Even this is not trivial. A teacher who begins the year with very dumb students can expect the largest gains in test scores. Statisticians have ways to compensate for this.

Evaluating teachers by testing students puts a lot of pressure on teachers and students. A few teachers have resorted to "cheating". Some cheating is blatant such as erasing responses. Others involve sending the poorer students on a "field trip" the day of the testing. A gray area is teaching to the test. Too much emphases on tests keep teachers from doing valuable projects or from helping students with their attitudes and personal problems.

At the college level, many poor teachers are kept because they bring in grant money for research. Some professors rely heavily on teaching assistants. It is important to state that being an expert in your subject matter does not make you a good teacher. I personally believe that people who are good at math should never teach it. Things that a math wizard considers obvious may not appear that way to a student struggling with the subject. The best people to teach math are those that struggled with it so they understand what some of their pupils are going through.

At the lower grades, teachers need to be aware of children who prefer seeing over hearing or doing over reading. As every child is different, teachers need to be able to relate and motivate a wide variety of young learners. Teaching is a stressful job and turnover is greater than most professions. There are no simple tricks to inspire others.

In any case, over time it gets around who are the good teachers. Unfortunately, salaries are not always related to teaching ability. Advanced degrees, continuing education, supply and demand, as well as office politics are involved. I give **teachers a 5** on the merit scale.

Lawyers

There was a time when lawyers only needed to pass the bar exam. Famous people who became lawyers without a formal education include Abraham Lincoln, Daniel Webster and Clarence Darrow. Now only the states of California, Washington, Virginia and Vermont do not require law school. These states require four years of apprenticeship under qualified supervision. However, most of these people do not pass the bar exams. In California, only a little more than half of all applicants pass the bar exam whereas less than one out of four pass it without a law degree.

Nearly all states require a bachelor's degree to apply for law school. Given that it doesn't matter what subjects you took, this seems like a strange requirement to me. When you seek a lawyer does it matter to you that the person studied biology or art history?

The average salary for a lawyer is about $136,000 per year. Unlike most professions, the range of salaries is quite large. Like most professions, I will grant that you must have merit to become a lawyer but do the best lawyers make the most money? The salary distribution for lawyers is bimodal. The mean salary looks high only because a sizable number of lawyers make $160,000 per year. Furthermore, if you went to law school you probably left with a lot of debt. The average law school costs about $34,000 a year. What type of lawyer you are affects your income. Copyright attorneys make more than family attorneys.

Ken Lopez of A2L Consulting says "From the outside of the industry, however, I think it's almost impossible to tell who is good. Good is almost entirely based on word-of-mouth, and world-of-mouth is usually affected by some form of confirmation bias. That is, people want to recommend a lawyer they've used before, since making that recommendation helps them reinforce the decision they made to hire that lawyer in the first place."

A successful lawyer nurtures his clients and spends time networking and marketing. Not surprisingly, the top skills for many types of lawyers are negotiating and persuasion. Unfortunately these skills are seldom good enough in law students to talk their professors into giving them a good grades. In other words, it is possible for an 'A' student at law school to become a mediocre lawyer.

The biggest problem I have with rating law high on the merit system is that where you went to law school and who you know seems to have a large effect on how much money you make. Furthermore, one successful class action suit can set up a lawyer up for life. Different types of lawyers need different abilities. Criminal lawyers need to be persuasive. Corporate lawyers need to be aware of the many laws and regulations that apply to the company. Supreme Court Justices need to know about precedence.

Whereas the best criminal lawyers win the most cases, personal injury lawyers apparently need good public relations and advertising. Furthermore, many a lawyer claims the work of a clerk or intern as his own. Overall, I give the **law profession a 4** on the merit scale.

STEM (Science, Technology, Engineering, and Math)

My father was an engineer and I worked for the Corps of Engineers. What I am going to say probably applies to the related occupations. My dad not only graduated from college as an engineer, he became a professional engineer later in life. In his day, he was credited with designing the world's largest packaging machine. It was for a lumber company in Canada.

I also worked at the Corps of Engineers. Engineers are practical people. Casual Friday was every day of the week. Dressing for success will not do you much good if your designs "don't hold water" (They design locks and levees). With data processing, if your program does not work correctly you make corrections until it does. According to Levees.org, failing flood walls cost the city of New Orleans $27 billion dollars. After Hurricane Katrina,

Bo Brothers rebuilt the Interstate 10 Bridge from New Orleans to Slidell for $803 million dollars. They finished early and the bridge is expected to last for 50 years.

The world needs people in the technology fields to improve transportation, communications and medical advances. Everything from robotics to a cheap solar stove for third world countries improves people's lives. These industries will take a variety of personalities and lifestyles if you are good at what you do. You can only cover up bad work for a short time. Airbags that injure drivers can make a billion dollar company go bankrupt.

Although I lumped STEM worker together, I am primarily talking about Engineering and technology. These fields stress the application of science and math. Those people in the pure sciences are recognized for theories and basic research. As such they rely on their peers for recognition. Published papers and awards, such as a Nobel Prize, distinguish the best scientists.

Of course it is possible to be a postal clerk like Albert Einstein until you publish a great discovery. Scientists make predictions from theory and it is not science if there is no way to prove a prediction is false. Einstein predicted gravity from a planet, bends light. This prediction has been verified to be true on several occasions.

Mathematician are a breed unto themselves. Hundreds of years ago, someone came up with the concept of an imaginary number that eventually found a practical application in electrical engineering. It is impossible to rate a mathematician if you cannot understand the math!

If you have school age daughters, have them consider a STEM career. Presently, less than 15% of STEM workers are female. Women can do math. Women can be creative. Women can work long hours if necessary. However, if a man gets angry at you, he will be over it the next day. (I never said I wasn't prejudiced.) I give the **STEM occupations an 8** on the merit scale. The reason why computer programmers get a higher score then STEM workers is because data processing people usually work alone. STEM workers are often part of a team, making it more difficult to determine who the best are.

Salesman

Salesmanship is based on the ability to manipulate the emotions of others; to dazzle and entertain. Selling doesn't have the prestige of doctors and lawyers. However, if you are <u>looking for a job where merit counts, this is the place to go</u>. I am strictly talking about salesmen who <u>work mostly on commission</u>. This includes car salesmen, insurance salesmen, and realtors. If you are a realtor, it doesn't matter how much time you put into a sale; if it falls through you receive no money. No physician loses any money if the patient dies. He gets paid for his effort to try and keep the patient alive. Having a college degree does not qualify you for a larger commission although it might give you an advantage in a sales manager position. Another advantage of being a good salesperson is that you can always get a job. If your company goes under, you still have your own personal record of achievement.

Are people born good salesmen or is it in the training? Probably some of both. Having an extroverted personality, a cheerful disposition and the gift of gab will help you succeed at selling. However, there are many books explaining various sales techniques. When I worked as a psychologist I was always impressed by the pharmaceutical salesmen. In fact, I recommend everyone who does counseling to study sales techniques. Having a perverse sense of humor, I deliberately put a picture of a sail boat in my office. As expected, the pharmaceutical salesmen picked up on the picture and asked if I sailed. With a deadpan look I responded "no, never had". Good sales people look for something you both have in common or something you enjoy. They will tell you how much they love the city where you grew up. They will call you by your first name as if you are an old friend. They will do something "just for you". Another sales trick is to point out a minor flaw in their product. This convinces you that this person must be honest because he put down his own product.

Bernie Madoff is an example of just how much money a good salesman can make. Of course he did it all illegally. If you choose selling, keep in mind that there is a fine line between salesman and conman. Pyramid schemes have always been popular among conmen. I remember attending a seminar on selling beauty products to women. Although the presenter did nothing illegal, he was good at convincing the audience that nothing was nobler than improving a woman's self-esteem than by making her beautiful. His sales technique was to convince you what a wonderful person you would be selling his product while cleverly alluding to the thousands of dollars you would make (not that there's anything wrong with that). So I give a **merit of 8 to salespeople on commission**. What keeps this job from being a 9 or 10 is that you may have to change jobs frequently as various products wax and wane. Remember The Music Man? There are no anvil salesmen anymore. Furthermore, you might have to compete against someone with no ethics (assuming you are ethical).

A major problem with being a salesman is that one of the biggest changes in recent years is the increased buying over the internet. Who would have guessed that big stores like Macy's and Penny's would be closing stores? Consequently, the typical store salesperson is especially in a tenuous position. Even a car salesman must be good enough to make a sale before the client leaves to "think it over." Otherwise, the salesman may have spent his time helping the client select a model so she can then get competitive prices over the internet.

Financial Advisors/Planners

If you do not live from hand to mouth, perhaps you need a financial advisor so you can put your extra cash to work for you. If you listen to the radio for very long you will certainly encounter a financial advisor who will make great promises. One thing that separates financial advisors from most occupations is that they will freely tell you what is wrong with other methods. Someone always seems to be discovering the "secret" to making money.

I attended the seminar of a well-known financial advisor with a popular radio program. He told the story of tracking 16 mutual funds companies. The first year 8 of them were successful (i.e., made more money than most).

The second year 4 of the 8 were again successful. The third year 2 of the 4 were successful. The fourth year 1 of the 2 was successful. The audience all wanted to know the name of that company that was successful four years in a row so they could invest. As a statistician I could only groan. It was highly likely that the company that did better than most for four years in a row was simply lucky. If you were to flip 16 coins 4 times, about 1 coin would have heads four times in a row.

I have also heard the story of a dart board that was doing as well as the experts at selecting stocks. My local television news likes to explain why stocks went up or down. The newscaster might explain the sudden rise in stocks to the recent news of reduced unemployment. However, when the stock market takes a dive three days later does that mean a lot of people were fired? In theory you could pick a good financial advisor by comparing track records over a ten year period. The fact that you will not see that in their advertisements speaks volumes.

In theory, a financial advisor should be a job that depends highly on merit. All financial advisors keep track of the percent profit made from their investments. Unfortunately, asking a financial advisor for their track record for the last ten years is likely to get you the run a round. They will tell you that there is no one answer as they "tailor" their investments to the needs and personalities of each client. As a statistician, I would say "that's fine, just give me the average percentage gain over the last ten years." At this point they might give you a number without any accompanying data or graphs to back it up.

I might be going out on a limb but I would say "salesmanship" is what makes a financial advisor rich. I have even heard a financial company mention how many Ph.D.'s they have working for them. I can tell you right now that these Ph.D.'s are thinking of ways the company can make money. Remember the housing crash of 2008? The best and brightest were thinking up ways to hide bad investments in with the good ones while keeping high credit ratings.

Speaking as a statistician, most models predict the future based on the past. This is not true knowledge, any amateur can do this. When the stock market was wildly fluctuating I created a buy/sell model base on "regression to the mean" (See Appendix 6). In other words, if the stock market (S&P) went up a certain percent in one day, I sold an "X" amount of stock. If the market went down a certain percent in one day, I bought an "X" amount of stock. After determining the best parameters to use based on past data, I used my model to predict how well I would do in the future. When the stock market was fluctuating widely, my model was doing well. Unfortunately, it did not stand the test of time. I needed different parameters to do well in the future when the stock market did not fluctuate so much. Furthermore, my model involved day trading. Day traders get a gambler's high. My model involved doing nothing for most of the time.

The best seminar I have ever attended was from Dr. W. Edward Deming, a physicist. He spoke of "true" knowledge. True knowledge allows you to make a prediction for something that has never happened before. Albert Einstein predicted that gravity bends light before he had any data to prove it. How many financial gurus predicted the housing collapse in 2008? Based on the movie "The Big Short" evidently a few bright people had true knowledge. They knew the housing market was about to collapse. How many financial advisors predicted many years on low inflation after 2008? Does that mean that even among the best and brightest only 1% have true knowledge?

I don't claim to be an expert in financial matters. I only know three things: One, diversify; two, don't touch your investments until an emergency or until you retire; and three, rebalance your assets occasionally. If you need a financial advisor, I have advice for you that I have never heard from any financial advisor. The day you put money into your individualized plan, check the S&P. Sometime in the future (2 to 5 years?) compare your earnings to what you would have received if you followed the S&P. If the S&P out-performed your plan, dump your financial advisor like a hot potato.

Note, there are different types of financial advisors. If you want to become one or choose to work with one you will need to know the differences. There are Certified Financial Planners, Chartered Financial Analysts, and Certified Fund Specialists to name a few. Fee only financial planners have a fiduciary obligation to act in your interests and not take fees for services they recommend. I might be prejudiced, but I can only give **financial planners a 3 on the merit scale**. If the best financial planners made the most money for their customers, they would begin their presentation with verifiable data that shows how much they outperformed the market over the last several years (deducting their fees of course).

Managers

Nearly everyone wants to be a manager because managers make the most money. But do they deserve it? Clearly not today. Why do I say this? Look at the salaries of CEO's of major companies relative to the average wage at that company. Whereas the average wage has gone up slowly over the years and has been stagnant for the last several years, CEO salaries including stock options and benefits has skyrocketed. According to the Economic Policy Institute, the compensation of the top 350 CEO's rose 997% from 1978 to 2014. During this same period the typical worker's pay rose 11%. Unless you believe the CEO's of today are immensely more talented than they were fifty years ago we have a problem. If you believe that managers should succeed on merit, you want to work for a company into profit sharing. Show me a company where the CEO takes a salary loss during a bad year if you believe this is a job that relies on merit. Of course I could probably show you two CEO's whose income went up during a bad year for every one whose income went down.

Management at the highest level seems to be a "good old boy" system. The board of directors are way too chummy with the executives. In my opinion, stock options should only exist as part of a profit sharing program that involves everyone.

I have a different problem with mid-management. Remember the "Peter Principle"? People get promoted to their level of incompetence. Take one good technical person and make her a manager. What do you get? It's a lose-lose situation. You now lost your best technical person and she needs to know how to deal with the people in the office who do their best to avoid work.

Everybody seems to have a story about bad management. The cartoon "Dilbert" has dozens of them. . I was actually fired from volunteer jobs – twice! These stories will tell you something about management.

The first volunteer job I was fired from was when I worked with the retarded while in graduate school at the University of Texas. Everything was going fine until they sponsored a dance in the evening. I attended the dance and had a good time interacting with the residents. The next day I showed up to volunteer I was called into the office. The man said I was being "let go" because I had brought a former resident to the dance. I knew who he was referring to but was not aware of any incident involving him. Furthermore, I wondered why the person in charge of the dance did not tell this former resident to leave. In any case, I did not bring up either of these topics. I simply told him the truth. One, I did not bring this man to the dance. And two, I had never seen him before in my life. For the next two minutes neither of us said a thing. I then got up and left never to return. It appeared that this man had a job to do and he was not going to go out of his way for a volunteer.

The second time I was fired from a volunteer job was when I worked at a church food pantry. The priest called me in to tell me I was no longer welcome at the food pantry. Three times I asked him "why?" He would not tell me. Evidently he had forgotten the words of Jesus who said "If your brother sins against you, go and tell him his fault" (Mathew 18:15).

In general, people skills are usually underrated as to their importance. People skills will not only help you in almost all occupations but will help you in your day to day life. People skills are critical for management. A relative of mine worked at a large company with a lot of highly skilled technical people. Unfortunately this was a company where a promotion meant becoming a supervisor. He said that many highly skilled technical people were washouts as managers. Chances are these self-motivated people do not have a clue on how to motivate someone else. Most of us learn people skills in kindergarten and grade school. It is not easy for an introverted technical person to change his or her personality.

Some people naively think than the job of a manager is telling people what to do. The first time a subordinate does not do as told, the manager is in a quandary. This manager probably grew up doing what his parents and teachers told him to do. Of course the manager could fire the person but this would be a considerable loss to the company in hiring and training costs. In all probability a manger facing this situation has a second problem – he does not realize that he is part of the problem. If you do not know how to motivate people and deal with various personalities, management is not for you.

Companies can avoid this problem in two ways. First, they can provide training to prospective managers. There are more classes in management than you can shake a stick at. I have had many of them. There is management by objectives, team manager, walk around manager, coaching manager, maximize diversity manager and priorities manager. Remember when management was out and leadership was in? I can only say from experience that if the instructor goes to the blackboard and draws four quadrants, get up and leave the room. She is surely about to demonstrate some simple-minded system. If you know about factor analysis, you know that there are very few orthogonal relationships.

Second, a company can test people for managerial/leadership skills. Probably a good test of managerial skills would involve role playing as opposed to book learning. At one time the Corps of Engineers used a measure of leadership developed by the Gallup Corporation. This measure created a lot of hostility among low scorers. I wrote a paper explaining how this measure had dubious validity (Appendix 7). Two researchers recommend a test of general mental ability along with a test of personal integrity to predict success for most jobs ("The Validity and Utility of Selection Methods in Personnel Psychology: Practical and Theoretical Implications of 85 Years of Research Findings", Schmidt and Hunter, Psychological Bulletin, 1998, Vol. 124, No. 2, 262-274).

I believe that management is its own skill. As such it would be quite possible that the manager of a highly technical department makes considerably less money than the people he supervises. Only a small number of businesses have tried this approach. I believe that Boeing tried this. One of the problems with the idea that management is its own job, is convincing people that, in my experience, it is easier to manage a group of computer programmers than a clerical pool. Consequently, if management were its own specialty then the manager of a clerical pool should make more money than the manager of computer programmers. I do not know of a single business where this is true! Overall, I give **management a merit score of 4**.

Entrepreneurs

If you are big on going as far as you can on your own merit, you might want to be your own boss. Creating your own business can be time consuming, plus you will probably need startup capital. If you have seen the TV program "Shark Tank", you realize you are not alone. The world is full of great ideas. According to Forbes, 8 out of 10 new businesses fail.   Clearly you need to be thick skinned to be an entrepreneur. Also, you are unlikely to have all of the skills to go it alone. You might be a great inventor but can you market? Can you build a prototype? Are you aware of all of the legal ramifications? Furthermore, timing is everything. You might have a great idea but be in the wrong place at the wrong time.

In addition to having perseverance, I do not recommend being an inventor if you have the slightest tendency toward paranoia. Invariably someone else has an idea similar to yours. Plus getting a patent is very involved. Of course a company with a lot of lawyers might actually steal your idea to justify your paranoia.

You might want to be your own boss doing something one person can do. If you can get a broker's license, you can be a one person realty. You could be a handyman, mow lawns, give massages, be a life coach, or sell a product over the internet.

My personal recommendation for making money is as follows. Buy the cheapest house on the market. Fix it up and sell it "by owner". Hopefully, you can do some of the fixing up yourself even if it is just painting. Use your profit to buy your next rundown house. Eventually you will be able to own two old houses. Here is where the real money comes. You rent one of the homes. Now you not only get rent money, you can deduct all of your repairs on your income tax. These repairs will allow you to raise the rent. This is a country where most of the laws favor the rich who create them. Renters get nothing whereas landlords get to deduct repairs, depreciation, interest on the loan, and any losses. Try to reduce your capital gains when possible. Years ago I read that real estate has created more millionaires than anything else. When we had a housing crisis and people could no longer afford their house payment, guess what? They had to rent!

At one time we were allowed to deduct our credit card interest on our taxes. Of course this encouraged people to overspend so it was eventually dropped. Did we learn anything from that experience? Evidently not. We had a housing crisis fueled by people who over bought. However, I do not see anyone clamoring to drop the tax break on mortgage interest.

Statisticians have something called a random walk, sometimes they refer to stochastic processes. Suppose you started at home and I tossed a coin into the air. Every time the coin landed on heads you walked north. Every time the coin landed on tails you walked south. Where would you be after 1000 throws? Probably near home. Now suppose every time the coin landed on heads you made $10,000 and every time it landed on tails you lost $10,000. Where would you be after 1000 throws? If you said near zero dollars you are wrong! Why? Because you can only lose so many dollars at which time you declare bankruptcy and start all over at zero dollars. On the other hand, there is <u>no limit</u> to how many dollars you can make.

Fortunately for you entrepreneurs, most people have a dreaded fear of bankruptcy. Worse yet, if they go bankrupt they quit the game. According to Politifact, Donald Trump's companies have filed for bankruptcy four times! No wonder he is poor. Whoops, did I say poor? I meant to say no wonder he is a billionaire. This is a man who doesn't give up.

Over the last 20 years there has been a lot of research on the psychology of money. First of all, economists long before 20 years ago talked about the utility of money. In other words, the value of a dollar is a lot to someone with no money. A dollar is almost meaningless to a millionaire. Once to have enough money to provide food and shelter for your family, the value of a dollar begins to drop. A more recent finding on the psychology of money is that a person will go across town to save $10 on a sweater but will not go across town to save $20 on a refrigerator.

My favorite study is the one where people are given the chance to bet on whether a light will come up red or green. Every time they guess correctly they win a dollar. Unknown to them, the light is programmed to <u>randomly</u> come up red 75% of the time and green 25% of the time. So what happens? Eventually most people will guess the red light 75% of the time and the green light 25% of the time. Unfortunately, this is not the best strategy. The best strategy is to <u>always</u> bet on the red light.

If I know so much about making money why aren't I rich? I took an early out from a government job to write a book and two complete musicals. I am not addicted to money. I may have to put out money to ever see one of my musicals performed.

I believe that more people are addicted to money than you might think. Day traders like to see quick gains. When I moved to Louisiana, the state was against gambling of any kind. Things changed when people from Louisiana went to the casinos in Mississippi and all the way to Florida for a Power Ball ticket. Unfortunately, it is not the rich people who foolishly buy lottery tickets. I tell people that the worst thing that can happen when you go to a casino for the first time is that you win.

I do not remember anyone saying this, but clearly Bernie Madoff was addicted to money. A normal person would have thought that $50 million dollars was enough. He could have planned an escape to South America. I do not believe Bernie subconsciously wanted to get caught any more than a heroin addict secretly wants to overdose and die. Even with the best of help, addictions are difficult to break. I have to add that various genetics predisposes someone to becoming addicted. If you are one of those rare people who decided you were done with smoking, quit and never smoked again, you are not disposed to becoming an addict. I do not make fun of obese people because my genetics does not allow me to get fat. "Will power" has never been a useful concept in psychology.

I actually considered becoming an entrepreneur in the 1990's. I created a program for matching up people according to their interests. I created a list of over 300 activities within 12 major categories such as Sports,

Outdoors, Hobbies and the Arts (See Appendix 8). An individual was allowed to choose his or her ten favorite interests from this list. Each interest was given a three digit code. Interests that match on the first digit get some credit. Interests that match on the first two digits get more credit and an exact match of all three digits get the most credit. Matches also considered age, education and zip code.

I had written the algorithm for matching interests in Microsoft Access for the personal computer. I also wrote the software in Oracle and 'C' for a mainframe. What makes this computer match different than today's competition is that it is not limited to a romantic connection. Singles could look for a friend of the same sex and couples could look for another couple.

My criticism of traditional romantic matching is given in my introduction: "Would you like to meet someone who is good looking, intelligent, rich, honest, dependable, sensitive, and affectionate? Who wouldn't? On the other hand, not everyone is looking for someone who loves to attend the theater when not out fishing." A 2012 research article by Finkle et al states "Regarding matching, no compelling evidence supports matching sites' claims that mathematical algorithms work— that they foster romantic outcomes that are superior to those fostered by other means of pairing partners" (Psychological Science in the Public Interest 13(1) 3 –66). I believe if you chose your mate on the basis on physical attraction, you are probably contributing to our high divorce rate. If you chose your mate on shared interests, you are probably still together.

Unfortunately, I never followed through with my idea for three reasons. One, I was afraid of the consequences of setting up a nice naïve person with a psychopath. Two, I had no marketing skills. Three, the personal computers at that time could not handle thousands of applicants. Why I never pursued this when personal computers became much more powerful, I do not remember. Today, this entire operation could be done over the internet with computers doing all of the work from accepting input to sending out the report. If you consider yourself to be an entrepreneur, be sure to read my appendices.

In summary, I give **entrepreneurs a high score** on the merit scale. As an entrepreneur you could become a multi-millionaire, you could go broke, or you could do both. Merit should not be your primary reason for choosing this occupational path. Someone needs to develop a test to see if this is a good fit for you.

Perhaps you are an inventor. Inventors are usually entrepreneurs. They need to take that same hypothetical test to see if they are in the right occupation. Have you ever watched "Shark Tank"? I have seen all four "sharks" pass up on a good invention because they did not like the presenter. If you think that as an inventor you did most of the work, you are in the wrong occupation. I thought that because so many people are in counseling, my book would be a hit. Who wouldn't want better counseling for less money? I was wrong. No regular publisher wanted my book. No college counseling department thought my book would be a good supplement to their textbooks on counseling. After two years of research creating my book, I sell about one copy every two months through Amazon e-books. After receiving a glowing review, I rarely sell a book (See Appendix 9). My problem is not the book. It is my complete ignorance of marketing. I needed an agent. If this book doesn't sell, I might pay someone to help me market it.

Protective Service People (Policemen, Firemen & Military)

Policemen, fire fighters and the military need to meet special qualifications for admittance. They are then given intense training. Some of the training is general/basic and some specific.

The average police academy last 19 weeks. An increasing number of police departments require some college. Federal police need to have a bachelor's degree. Many colleges offer a degree in criminology/criminal justice. Additional training can lead to promotions. In addition to performance reviews, some police departments have promotion exams. A lot of policemen make extra money by working extra hours at their regular job or a side job.

You need a high school education and 3 to 4 months of training or more to become a fireman. You will probably go through a 6 to 12 month probationary period. You will need to maintain excellent physical condition. Some colleges offer an associate or bachelor's degree in fire science.   One way to improve your earning potential is to also become an Emergency Medical Technician (EMT) or paramedic.

A career in the military is usually chosen for reasons unrelated to rising to the top. The military offers job security, travel, medical care and possible training in various specialties. Best of all, the military offers early retirement. When I lived in San Antonio, retired military often took on a job for extra money. If you are upward mobile, you would need to first get accepted to one of the military academies. Military academies are extremely difficult to get in but they offer free tuition and a guaranteed job. Of course, that job might mean war.

To become a policeman or fireman you must have a clean record. Even beyond the probation period, those that can't cut it are dismissed. Once in, you are still subject to periodic evaluations. Of course, you must maintain that clean record. Firemen go to the gym I attend. I can verify that these people are in great physical shape. Policemen make about $53,000 per year. Firemen make about $5,000 less. Salaries, in general, are related to the size of the city with large cities paying the most. However, once in a protective occupation, years of service are probably more related to salary than excellence of performance. Of course, special acts of bravery can receive special commendations.

The Peter Principal is a potential killer for these action oriented people. Administrative talent and leadership skills can be far removed from the grit of their daily activities. As mentioned, the military has solved this problem with academies that serve as colleges for planning, administration and leadership. The police departments have special training for detectives. FBI training and similar agencies would be for the highly qualified.

Whereas incompetent CEO's often hang onto their positions of power with their stock in the company, the "Good Old Boy" system and blaming others, people's lives are at stake among the protective services. Consequently, one bad decision involving lives or property can lead to a person's demotion or removal.

In summary, I would give **protective service people a 5 on the merit scale**. The services are good for eliminating the poor performers but the bulk of the service people are mostly rewarded for years of service.

Personal Services (Hair Dressers, Barbers, Masseurs)

Before to the 20th century, with the exception of the wealthy, women took care of their own hair and beauty. In 1888, Martha Harper developed her own hair tonic and opened a hair salon. In the 1950's and 60's, beauticians had specialized products and could color hair.

Like the protective services, most people involved in the personal services need some type of license. Cosmetologists earn about $28,000 per year with much variation. Barbers make about the same with less variation. You need to attend an accredited school of cosmetology. Spas and dermatologists often employ estheticians who do various skin treatments. Aestheticians must complete a minimum of 300 hours of training and pass both a written and hands-on exam. They make about $33,000 per year. A medical aesthetician requires additional training and can make about $44,000 per year. They often work with electronic/laser devices.

Masseurs, also called massage therapists require a minimum of 300 hours of training. An advantage of being a masseur is that you can be self-employed. They make about $37,000 per year. Massage is also known to relieve aches and pains in muscles knotted by anxiety, posture, tension, and repetitive motion injuries, as well as soothe the nervous system and bolster the immune and lymphatic systems. There are many types of massages including Swedish, Hot Stone, Deep Tissue, Shiatsu, and Sports. The popular Swedish massage has five basic strokes. Each type of massage is for a different purpose. The Deep Tissue massage may help someone with chronic pain whereas the Sports massage might focus on a particular muscle group.

Somewhat surprisingly, prices vary considerably for haircuts and other beauty services. It has been my perception that the price you pay relates more to the environment than the person applying the treatment. I go to a "hole in the wall" and get my haircut by an older man. Consequently, I pay very little. I could go to a mall and pay more. I could go to a specialty shop that mostly caters to women and pay considerably more. I have gone to a variety of places for a haircut and have not noticed any significant difference in quality. However, I expect this is not true for women. However, you still pay for the building. Spas are known for their elaborate décor. I expect some women dress up for these services.

One advantage of the specialty shop is that you need an appointment. If your time is valuable, this may be the way to go. Once retired, I did not mind waiting in a first come, first serve setting as I brought along my own reading material.

It only makes sense that you should pay more for the "royal treatment." Some personal service workers have a knack for making you feel important. They are happy to see you. They ask about your child in college or your last vacation. They usually have the gift of gab and if they are really good, they know when you prefer peace and quiet. Don't we all like to be pampered?

Most people in the personal services work in a salon or spa. However, many people rent a space/chair. Consequently, developing a clientele is important. In this case, you are more likely to make what you are worth. Obviously, personality is important in addition to job skills.

Cosmetologists work with a variety of chemical products. Some of these chemicals are potentially dangerous such as toluene and formaldehyde.

A principle advantage with being a masseur is that success is primarily measured by how much better the clients feel after treatment. Consequently, if you have that special touch you should be able to charge more and get word of mouth recommendations.

It appears that some shops cater to women and others to men. The shops and spas that cater to women usually have a variety of services. Massage parlors for men seem to be often run by Asian women. I have been told that the women that know how to "take care of a man" get large tips.

I can only give a **merit score of 4 for personal services** as so many other factors than individual talent contribute to financial advantage. Plus, with a few exceptions, the average person will only pay so much for these services.

Food Services (Chefs, waiters and bartenders)

Waiters and waitresses rely heavily on tips. Throughout the United States, their typical wages are only a little over $20,000 per year. Tips are considerably higher in metropolitan areas as well as resort areas. For unknown reasons, people in Boston and San Francisco tip more than those in Minneapolis or Seattle. According to SimplyHired.com the average salary for a waiter in Houston is $49,000 a year. A table captain at a top of the line restaurant can make from $60,000 to $90,000 per year.

Being a waiter or waitress is hard work. Being pleasant to unpleasant people can be emotionally taxing. In addition to being friendly and polite, you need a good memory, stamina and efficiency. Most people would consider the times (i.e., hours of the day and days of the week) that food service workers have to put up with are less than desirable. Given the hours and the stress, alcohol and drug use is a potential job hazard. On the positive side, this can be a good part-time or second job.

Given that tips usually represent a proportion of the total cost of the meal, a waiter would prefer to work at an upscale restaurant. So how does a great waiter at a Denny's restaurant work himself up to a position at an upscale restaurant? I do not really know but I find it highly unlikely that a good recommendation from the Denny's manager is sufficient. My guess is who you know is more important. Of course an upscale restaurant has high standards and I expect many novices do not cut it. Consequently, a person who is persistent and can work under conditions that are hectic and with unreasonable people (customers and bosses) might eventually have a chance. Because of the high standards, I expect that workers at expensive restaurants generally provide excellent service. Sadly enough, we have all encountered excellent waiters and waitresses at low budget dinners and the best we can do is give a tip that is generous for that establishment.

According to the Bureau of Labor Statistics, bartenders make about the same as waiters. Sources on the internet believe this is a great underestimate. One such source says that bartenders make $230 for a 10 hour shift. Allegedly, a bartender in Manhattan made $1,000 per night. More realistically, bartenders in high class bars on the east and west coast can make $500 per night.

Similar to waiters, bartenders need to be friendly, pay attention to details, and work fast. Although you can learn with on the job training, it might be difficult to get a job without a certificate from a state licensed school of bartending. These schools usually run one or two weeks. Bartending is a job with a high turnover rate. Note that bartenders have a high ethical, if not legal, responsibility for clients who are clearly intoxicated.

Bartending seems to attract gregarious people who like what they are doing. Some are counselors and confidants while others are entertainers. I would imagine that encouraging a regular clientele would increase a bartenders tips. With several bartenders, tips are likely to be shared.

Chefs make about $63,000 per year with much variation. Chefs are entirely different animals. Their reputation is generally built up over the long haul. Of course there are the schools of chiefdom that insure a good start for someone lucky enough to gain admission. Culinary schools/institutes can be at least as expensive as a regular college degree.

Food critics have some impact on the reputation of chefs but not as much as word of mouth or should I say taste of mouth. Unfortunately, chefs are a little like football coaches. They are at the top one day and gone the next. The stereotype that good chefs are temperamental makes for good television and poor business.

When it comes to tipping food service workers, some customers give the quality of service a serious consideration. However, I believe that most people stick close to the going rate and will have pity on a worker who appears to be having a bad day. I give **food service workers a 4 on the merit scale with chiefs getting a 6.**

Tradesmen (Plumbers, Electricians, and Carpenters)

The trades have prospered for a few hundred years. While people with college degrees are looking for jobs, tradesmen are in demand. The average plumber makes close to $50,000 a year with some making considerable more. Electricians and carpenters make similar wages. To be fully qualified tradesman (journeyman), you first have to work three or more years as an apprentice. You can then take an exam to be licensed by the state. After working several years as a journeyman, you can then apply to the state to take an exam to be a master plumber, electrician or carpenter.

The trades have many things in common. One, you will probably driving a truck with various materials. Two, you will probably work more than an eight hour day. Three, you can work for yourself. Even if you work for a company you probably will not have a retirement program. Four, a few "bad apples" make many people wary of your services. Both plumbers and electricians deal with emergency situations.

As a plumber you need to be strong. You will have to deal with large tubs and water heaters as well as pipes that are difficult to disconnect. Worst of all is dealing with dirt and grime as well as human waste. You might also be dealing with the cold such as working below a house. At times you might need to crawl in tight spaces.

As an electrician you have to deal with the dangers of working with electricity. You will need to understand architectural drawings and schematics. You must be familiar with relays, switches, circuit breakers and other electrical devices. You will need fine motor skills to splice, thread, and connect various color coded wires.

As a carpenter you work with power tools. A carpenter needs good spatial ability and hand-eye coordination. Working on construction projects could put you as various heights. Some carpenters specialize in furniture and cabinets. Carpenters have high job satisfaction, probably because they can see their work.

In many cases, you can see the work of a tradesman. Does the toilet flush? Does the fan work? How do the corners of the crown molding look? Did the person clearly explain what he was about to do? Did he clean up when through? Is the work guaranteed? Was the job finished on schedule? Were any extra charges tacked on?

Clearly, everything that runs on electricity has to work. So how does a person know if their electrician is one of the best? I had an electrician redo my switches because I wanted the first switch to always do the room lights and not a fan or heater. One plumber might be faster than another but if the job costs the same it matters little to me. Some of a carpenter's work is readily visible such as the mantel for a fireplace. Other work such as on beams and walls are not. Fortunately, there are several rating services such as Angie's List, Home Advisor, Better Business Bureau, and sites like Google that gives stars to most of the trades. Plus, you can always get a recommendation from a friend or neighbor.

The more often you use tradesmen, the better you become at judging their quality. Tradesmen who are good are in demand, especially by general contractors. I give **tradesmen a 7** on the merit scale.

Construction/Contractors

Closely related to the trades is the construction industry. Cities are constantly expanding. New buildings call for new infrastructure. Old infrastructure needs replacement and repair. I found myself a builder for a new home. I got his name by word of mouth and inspected and spoke with the owners of some of his previous work. This is a job where the qualifications differ from state to state. In general, you do not need a college degree although some colleges offer a degree in construction management. You will need several years of experience and pass an exam to get a state license. You will need to purchase insurance and possibly a bond. In addition to knowing the trades, you will have to have the skills to run a business. A general contractor oversees a variety of construction although you could specialize in areas such as roofing, masonry, or heating and air conditioning.

There appears to be no limit to the amount of money you can make in construction. General contractors earn about $90,000 per year but the salaries vary from $50,000 to $150,000. Contractors make 10 to 20 percent of the total cost. Big jobs for cities and states often pay bonuses for on-time work.

There are plenty of headaches watching your home go up. The contractor lives with these day after day. He is reliant on a variety of subcontractors and the varying price of materials. This is not an 8 hour, 5 days a week occupation. This is not a job for a worrier or somewhat with thin skin. However, the rewards are great, not only in money but in seeing the end products of your work. The biggest handicap to this career is the ups and downs of the general economy and insuring you can get the people you need to complete the job in a timely manner. I give **construction an 8** on the merit scale. The best always find work.

Transportation

Transportation is another huge industry from taxi cabs to airline pilots to truck drivers. Obviously I cannot lump the previous jobs together. An airline pilot with advanced training can make over $100,000 per year (median about $115,000). The bigger the airline, the higher the salary. To obtain a commercial pilot's certificate you will need to pass several tests as well as have 250 hours of flight time.

A truck driver can make about $45,000 per year. Having a commercial driver's license can earn an extra $20,000. This is a job for people who like the open road and working alone although some truckers work in pairs.

Cab drivers attract foreigners with minimal skills whereas there never seem to be enough drivers for the big rigs. Rates are strictly controlled for cab drivers so your merit might only get you a slightly bigger tip. Taxi drivers make from $30,000 to $40,000 per year. Uber driving is a good part time job for many people.

Whether a cab or a truck, you make money by putting in the hours. A good safety record insures your career as a truck driver. Plus a good safety record as well as fuel efficiency can get you bonuses. An owner/operator of a big rig can give you an income of over $250,000 per year. However, repairs and other expenses can be considerable.

Boat captains make from $30,000 to $100,000 per year with the average around $60,000. The captain of a large cruise vessel can earn $150,000 per year whereas the captain of a cargo liner might make about $110,000 per year. For larger ships you will need several weeks coast guard approved training and pass an exam. You will need to know CPR and first aid and have from 90 days to a year of service. Similar to driving a truck, your job will require you to be away from home for many days at a time. Of course you will have to live near the job. Presently, Louisiana has the most boat operators with over 7,000 followed by Florida and Texas with nearly 3,000 operator each.

Transportation jobs includes logistics which I will not rate. Driving jobs eliminate the poor drivers but do little to significantly improve the wages of the good drivers. I give **driving a 3** on the merit scale.

News Media

News is now available 24/7. We have television, radio, newspapers and magazines. News reporters earn about $45,000 per year although some make considerably more. Whereas the average salary of a news anchor is over $80,000 per year, the news anchors of the major television networks make in the millions. Sports anchors make about $60,000 per year although popular ESPN analysts make over a million. Meteorologists earn from $40,000 to $140,000 per year with the average being a little over $90,000.

Jobs in the news are often competitive, harried, and constantly changing. For better or worse, paper is on the way out. News will soon be available only on an electronic device. As I alluded to earlier, news has become entertainment. If the television news media only cared about merit, one in three newscasters would be overweight. Consequently, just as I am unable to rate artists on the merit scale, I can no longer rate news casters. The days of Robert Cronkite are over. If you can appeal to a small but loyal group of listeners, you can have a place in the news media.

With a degree in communications you can work in public relations, human resources or advertising. Best you have a specialty in a technical area such a film production if you want to excel on merit. God help those who major in history or journalism. **No rating for news media.**

Farming

Most of our ancestors were farmers. In 1870, about half of our population was employed by agriculture. Today, it less than 2 percent. Over the last 30 years the average age of a farmer went from 50 to 58 years old. Becoming a first time famer has huge start-up costs. Surprisingly, the Department of Agriculture reported that in 2017 the number of famers under the age of 35 is actually increasing. Most (69%) of these farmers had college degrees. According to the *New York Times* (August 9, 2014) "the median farm income was negative $1,453 in 2012". Presently, the United States has a little over 2 million farms. Corn and soybeans are the biggest crops. Organic farming is on the rise.

Livestock farmers seem to make a bit more money. Poultry and cattle farmers earn about $70,000 per year but incomes varies considerably depending on the size of the operation. Livestock farmers must consider many expenses when calculating their earnings for the year. Some of these expenses include the costs of feed, fuel, supplies, insurance, veterinary services, waste removal, and equipment maintenance or replacement. If they have paid help they might need someone to help them with their taxes.

Livestock farmers need to know about nutrition and disease control. Some have degrees in animal science. Like crop farming, the hours are long and the work is hard. Livestock farmers must be aware that some diseases that can be transmitted from animals to humans such as ring worm, salmonella and even hepatitis and tuberculosis.

Farming is a tough life. Fortunately, today they have modern machinery for planting, irrigation, and harvesting. Still it is possible to have an early freeze, a hail storm or too much rain. Even if a farmer has a bumper crop he might discover that the price is low given that others have had the same "luck".

If you love the outdoors, animals, eating fresh food, and being close to family – farming may be your cup of tea (or fresh milk). Also, if you are a survivalist, farming allows you to be self-sufficient. Of course I am talking about small family farms. Large corporate farming is slowly but steadily growing. You choose farming for the lifestyle, not to demonstrate your merit. Consequently, I give **farming a 3**.

The Corporate Job

There are very few books helping people choose a career probably because of stating the obvious. If you are good with math consider the sciences. If you have a way with words consider a job with a lot of writing. If you are good with your hands you might select a trade. If you are good with people consider sales or management.

There are many books on how to succeed on the job, any job. The following 20 traits will help you succeed in business:

(1)   Build strong relationships
(2)   Act professional
(3)   Take initiative
(4)   Promote yourself
(5)   Develop multiple skills *
(6)   Be honest
(7)   Under promise, over deliver
(8)   Do critical thinking *
(9)   Show dedication
(10)   Be positive
(11)   Collaborate
(12)   Avoid gossip
(13)   Learn the business *
(14)   Make your boss look good
(15)   Have a competitive spirit
(16)   Socialize
(17)   Make yourself indispensable *
(18)   Be proactive
(19)   Manage expectations
(20)   Be a team player

The items with a star are related to merit. As you can see, success on most jobs has more to do with social skills and character than the ability to do what you were hired to do.

There are also a few books on finding the right corporate environment that suits your personality and values. Some companies respect family values and are lenient regarding family emergencies. Other companies offer free gym memberships. Some companies use teams to do most of the work. The federal government offers security by rarely laying off or firing employees.

Back in the days of IBM, men wore suits and ties and pretty much stuck to their desks. You were told when you could have a break or go to lunch. Workers at Google get free food including coffee and drinks. They get a gym with free fitness classes. They can ride the Google bus to work. You can even bring your dog. In the old days, you tried to make your boss happy. Today, your boss tries to make you happy.

One popular buzzword is the "corporate culture". The simplest definition of culture is the unwritten rules of a group of people. For example, if most people come back to their desk late from lunch that would be an unwritten rule. Do the workers general go right home after 8 hours of work or is a forty plus workweek expected? Dress code is often unwritten such as whether a man wears a tie or does not wear one. Some businesses encourage free expression of ideas. Some businesses like a person who does not make waves. I wrote something about what cultural change is for the Corps of Engineers (See Appendix 10).

Does your business promote the best? Do they offer special recognition for special achievements? Do they recognize teams more than individuals? Do they offer profit sharing? Do they provide the training you need to advance? There is **no way to give a merit score to corporations** in general as they vary widely on how far you can go on merit alone. Some companies reward loyalty/longevity more than accomplishments. Success in other companies depends on relationships and attitude.

Individual Sports

Competitive people like sports. Consequently, all sports are pretty high on the merit scale, especially individual sports. Still, some sports are higher than others. I love the Olympics. However, I can only give **ice skating an 8**. Ice skating scores rely on human judges. Judges all have prejudices; some known and some unknown. Some judges favor certain countries or skaters. I remember Scott Hamilton receiving a gold medal after a performance with a noticeable flaw. Everyone loves Scott Hamilton and it was his time. For better or worse, skating judges seem to know all of the top skaters. If a judge has seen a skater do a certain trick perfectly the last ten times, it appears to me that the judge is more lenient than on a newcomer. Skating involves both skill and artistry. Some judges reward originality and some do not. Plus, judging artistry seems to me to have quite a bit of subjectivity.

Diving and gymnastics are other individual sports that depends on judges. In an effort to be fair, the highest and lowest scores are eliminated. Like skating, the difficulty of the performance effects the final score. Fortunately, there is good agreement on difficulty ratings.

It is best to follow a poor performer than a good performer. This is known as contrast effect. In general, the performer who is up last has an advantage over the first performer, even if the order is chosen at random. Consequently, if performers are up more than once, the order should be reversed to compensate for this effect. I was in gymnastics in college. It was tradition that the poorest performers went first and the best performer went last. Consequently, it was hard to be up first and surpass those who follow unless someone makes an obvious mistake. One of the things that skating and gymnastics have in common is that a fall keeps you from getting any kind of medal. Consequently, athletes considered the best can still lose.

My rule is that if you are a true competitor, you should avoid a sport that involves judges. Does this mean I would give swimming a 10? In swimming the first person to touch wins and major mistakes are rare. Actually I would give **swimming a 9**. Why? Because it is possible that your competitor is on enhancing drugs. Swimming, bicycling and baseball have all had scandals involving doping. Swimmers can win races by hundredths of a second. Therefore, it would make sense for a swimmer to find something he can ingest that is not on the banned list.

Skiing is a sport I enjoy watching. I also enjoy skiing for fun. I cannot imagine enhancing drugs that would make you a better skier. Skiing is a sport of finesse as well as muscle. I was told by a ski instructor that women are faster at learning how to ski than men because the men try to muscle their turns. He also said that the men eventually pass up the women when they get to the hills that are very steep as males do not like to show fear. I give a merit score of **8 for skiing.** I cannot give higher because of varying snow conditions beyond the skier's control. Sometimes the conditions of the course are best for the first skier and sometimes it favors a later skier.

Does any sport deserve a merit score of 10? Probably not. Not only does every athlete have a bad day but random events related to weather and field conditions are possible. **Individual track and field events come the closest to a 10**. If you can throw a javelin further than anyone else you should be a winner. Furthermore, given more than one opportunity to throw the javelin decreases the influence of random events.

Does anyone doubt that Usain Bolt is the fastest man in the world? As it turns out, in 2011, Justin Gatlin ran the 100 meters in 9.45 seconds, beating Usain Bolt's fastest time by .13 seconds. On the other hand, Usain Bolt has 9 Olympic gold medals in running events. To be accurate you might say that Usain Bolt is <u>consistently the fastest man in Olympic competition</u>.

Team Sports

Most people love team sports – football, baseball, basketball, hockey, soccer. When watching a team sport such as football, commentators like to show statistics on individuals. For example, they may point out that the quarterback has a 62% passing completion rate for this season. Does this make the quarterback a better passer than one with a 58% completion rate? Remember, this is a team sport. If the quarterback bounces a football off the chest of one of his receivers, this is considered a miss, even if your grandmother could have caught the ball. Likewise, a running back can average more yards per carry if he has good blockers.

Good professional athletes are rewarded with big salaries. Sometimes an athlete does not shine until he aligns with the right team. The top athletes seem to excel wherever they go. Unfortunately, injuries can sideline the best of athletes. Someone once told me that being a professional athlete is the last thing you want to be if you value a healthy body. Old age for a professional athlete brings on arthritis, Parkinson's disease (from concussions?) and various aches and pains from old injuries.

I have never understood the point of career totals in passing, running and touchdowns. Clearly, these figures are highly dependent on how many years of play the person has. It seems to me that the only figures that count are averages per game. If a player hangs on too long, these averages might actually go down over time.

One of the things I personally dislike about baseball is its tremendous reliance of good pitching. If your pitcher can throw a no-hitter, the worst your team can do is come up with a tie. I prefer little league where you can only have a strike called on you if you swing the bat and miss. For the youngest little leaguers, the pitcher is on the same side as the batter. That will give the fielders something to do!

To make football competitive, the NFL allows the poorest performing teams to have the early picks of potential players for the next season. Unfortunately, colleges do not work that way. The most promising high school football players seek out a college with an outstanding record on the field. By playing for a top college team, a player increases his chances for being a draft pick for a professional team. Consequently, when a top football college does well on the field, it is difficult to tell how much credit goes to the coaching staff.

I have seen colleges recruit staff from other colleges that have consistently winning teams. I always thought a better strategy was to recruit staff from colleges that did not do well until their coaching staff changed. To me, this is a better indication that the coaching staff are the ones that made the difference. We have all seen coaches fired after three years of losing, even though these same coaches had winning teams previously. I can see coaches getting better over time with more experience but it seems unlikely that a coach suddenly forgot how to win.

The Arts

I have never understood competition and awards in the arts. I always thought that the arts (i.e., drama, music, dance, and painting) were personal expressions of the inner feelings of the people involved. In other words, there is no right or wrong. There is no better or worse. There are only degrees of liking or disliking.

As a musician I see my role as bringing to life a musical composition by projecting my unique personality, interpretations, and feelings into any solo piece. Consequently, barring any obvious mistakes, choosing a winner becomes a personality contest. Therefore, if my personality is not in the mainstream, my only hope of winning a music contest is to become "someone else". Philosophically, this appears to be a dead-end if the arts exist primarily for individual expression. In fact, all of the arts have pioneers whose work is initially rejected only to become in vogue at a later date.

Let's look at the movies. As far as I can tell, there are only three metrics that count. One, how many people saw the movie? Two, how much did they like it? And Three, how much money did it make?

Critics can say what they like about a movie. Everyone has an opinion. What qualifications does it take to be a movie critic? This is not a rhetorical question. I really do not know the answer. Why would I care what the distinguished Academy says about a movie? The best thing I can say about the Academy Awards is that it is helpful to people who never watch a movie until it has been out for at least a year. If you had already seen the movie, why would you care about someone else's opinion?

I can understand People's Choice. Even though I have my own individual preferences, I like to know what most people think. On the other hand I do not see the need to give an award based on the people's choice. Performances that people love are money makers. Why doesn't the industry just use that information to help plan their next movie?

Awards in the arts seems to be another case of giving more to people who already have too much. If I had a job that paid me over a million dollars a year, I could get by without a little statue on my mantel. I like going into a fast food restaurant and seeing a picture of the Employee of the Month. Sure, it makes no logical sense that the best person in the month of January fell short in February, but it is nice to get some recognition when you make so little over minimum wage. I remember the days when banks made people vice presidents and gave them other titles when they could not afford pay increases.

I expect that most people are against contests in the arts for young people. Displays of art work and piano recitals are great for young people. Awards only discourage the many losers.

If you are going to have a competition in the arts, you should do it right. I enjoy the International Piano Competition in New Orleans but they certainly do **not** do it right. Here is what I suggest:

(1) Take a tip from The Voice, <u>do not allow the judges to see the competitors</u>.

   (A) First of all, this will eliminate the obvious prejudices such as Asians are technical players and men are more forceful.

   (B) More importantly, it will avoid being influenced by body language. When watching, it is difficult to hear the sensitivity of a piano player if her body is not swaying all over the piano as she plays. There is even a story about how one critic who only heard the record (Isaac Stern?) commented on the sensitivity of the player while the critic who saw him play said just the opposite. Evidently, Isaac Stern did not sway as he played.

   (C) When you see the same player perform a different piece later, you could be influenced by the previous performance.

(2) Avoid position effects. As I said earlier, if you were to take all contests and look at position, you would find that people who go toward the end do better than people who go early. When people perform twice, you need to reverse their position. This needs to be done even when you need to watch the performance such as in skating.

(3) Have each performer do the same piece plus a chosen one.

(4) Make sure that there is a reasonable agreement among the judges. For example, if two judges were

to rank order the contestants and had perfect agreement, the two scores would have a correlation of 1.00. No agreement between the judges would be a 0.00 correlation. Anyone can add up scores to produce a winner but these scores have no meaning if judges do not have a reasonable agreement, roughly a correlation of .7 or higher.

Note that agreement among judges will be greater when judging amateurs than for professionals. Judging the performance of first year pianists would be fairly easy. Accurately comparing the performances of professional pianists is very difficult. Professionals make few mistakes which leaves the judges to consider something as vague as interpretation and artistic merit. The appearance of being a great piano player can be enough to give someone an edge.

Personally, I am at a lost as to how someone can judge abstract art. I can tell if a landscape painting evokes feelings as actually being there. With any form of abstract art all I have is a feeling. This is not to say that art critics, who know so much more about art than I, do not have validity. However, I do know that some works of art are appreciated more and some less over time as opinions and circumstances change.

One problem with judging the arts is that there are so many niches. In dance competitions contestants usually have to do a variety of dances. In football, you will never see a quarterback hike the ball. Furthermore, an artist does not have to do portraits, landscapes and abstract art to get recognition. Singing competitions might involve several different styles but you are unlikely to hear opera, jazz and pop from each contestant. Musicians might play two or three different instruments but rarely more.

Some performers have great showmanship but less than stellar performance. The best seem to have both talent and showmanship. Elvis swayed his hips. Michael Jackson did a moon walk. Mick Jagger moves like a man on amphetamines. Kiss had recognizable outfits and tongues. Other performers are either lucky or know how to make money with what talent they have. We will seldom have number one songs like the "Hit Parade" had in the 1950's because so much of the market is presently controlled by teenagers.

When I was trying to market a book, I discovered that nearly all publishing companies send you a reply. Of course, most of these replies are form letters telling you that your work might be wonderful but it is not for them.

I have also tried to market two musicals. I should put market in quotes. I am not seeking any remuneration, I am only hoping that some community theater would like to perform one of my musicals. My first musical, "The Visitor", is an old fashioned musical comedy that takes place in a psychiatric hospital. Eight different people have solos. I had someone interested in producing this musical. After getting my hopes up, he later told me that it would be too expensive to produce. That is when I wrote my second musical, "The Twenties", which contains four young people, a soprano, alto, tenor and bass, and an older man who was the narrator. This musical could be done in a small theater. Whereas my first musical features a variety of made up psychiatric characters, my second musical has many references to Bix Beiderbeck, the most fascinating musician I have ever read about.

Unlike publishing companies, legitimate theaters rarely give you any feedback regarding inquiries. I have been told the theater is an example of where you need a track record before they will do your work but you cannot get a track record unless someone takes a chance on you. Would it help me if I got involved in Community Theater in some capacity and made a few connections? As you know, I am a big believer in feedback. It is possible that I do not know the right people but it is also possible that my work is not up to par.

My advice is: If you are interested in the arts, God only knows what you will need to succeed. **In the arts, merit plays a part, but often a small part.**

Merit in School

In the future, I believe a college degree will be replaced by internet courses, standardized tests, and specific employment tests. In 1950, 6.2% of adults 25 or older had a bachelor's degree or higher. This percent rose to 24.4% by the year 2000. Since the 1990's, cable television has programs on history, science and geography. One can now take classes over the internet as well as research various topics. At the same time that more people are attending college, the cost of a college education is rising more than the cost of living. Furthermore, many graduates have discovered that a college degree does not automatically lead to a job, or a job that makes their investment worthwhile. In other words, there seems to be less need for a college education now than in the 1950's.

For the time being, many occupations still require a college degree(s). A federal job gives you credit for a degree(s) even if you have forgotten everything you learned. Fortunately, schools, in general, rank high on the merit system. You excel in school by homework, essays, special projects, grades and standardized tests. I give **schools an 8 on merit** at this time.

Standardized tests are important because schools vary considerably. When I was involved in hiring, one of our applicants went to both the University of New Orleans and Harvard. His GPA was a full grade lower at Harvard, probably reflecting their strict admission standards.

Most colleges look at ACT or SAT scores. When I was in school, no one studied for these tests. Furthermore, there once was a time when public service meant something when applying to college. Now most high schools require it.

Many students who get a high or perfect test score have studied specifically for these tests. Both the ACT and SAT have an essay section to reflect writing ability. Even writing the perfect paragraph can be learned. I believe the essay section should include "off the wall" questions to demonstrate a person's ability to think on his or her feet. These questions should last no longer than one year so no one could study for them. Examples of "off the wall" questions would be:

(1) What would you recommend to get Republicans and Democrats in Congress to cooperate with each other?
(2) If you wanted to be a physician, would you be in a team sport in high school and why?

(3) If you could change one tax law, what would it be and why?

(4) How would you lower crime in the United States?

(5) How important is math for someone in the arts?

There is no end to questions that require independent thinking. I would hope that our merit scholars have already done this on their own. When I was the job interviewer at Waterborne Commerce Statistics Center, it became clear that there was little point in asking someone to list their strong and weak points. Most applicants had pat answers.

Why Merit?

I have spent a lot of time analyzing which jobs you can advance to the top on merit alone. I have not discussed why this might be important to you. Let me start with one of the findings of a 2013 World Happiness Study. Given their socioeconomic status, the study found that Asians were not as happy as you might expect and Hispanics were happier than expected. While in San Antonio I belonged to a chapter of the American Statistical Society and also played with "L'Orchestra Dominguera", a Hispanic musical group. Indeed I did find that the musicians who were barely eking out a living to appear happier than a group of well-educated statisticians.

Every high school has students who study hard to get into the best colleges where they study hard to get into graduate school so they can become doctors, lawyers, engineers and other scientists. I am not aware of any longitudinal studies of these people to see what their lives are like as adults. I am guessing that many of these people work long hours at their occupation, not because they need to but out of habit. When I was in high school I had friends like this. They all made the National Merit Society whereas I did not. They continued to make good grades in college. I made a 'C' in a calculus class because I refused to memorize integration formulas. Fortunately I made it to graduate school on my GRE scores, not my grades.

The bottom line is that an occupation based on merit is important to me because I do not want to work long hours. I want to rise to the top of my chosen occupation on quality, not quantity. If I were an independent psychotherapist or a physician I would work four days a week, nine hours per day. For our safety the Accreditation Council for Graduate Medical Education has limited the number of work-hours to 80 hours per week. That should keep physicians from over working! While I would have preferred to work as a psychologist, the federal government let me rise near the top (a GS-14) on a 40 hour week with 5 weeks of vacation per year.

Ever since my first job I have played my trumpet with some form of musical group. I have been composing music since I was in high school. This is the third book I have written. I have also written several humorous monologues (see Appendix 11 for an example) and several letters to the editor (see Appendix 12). I still visit a lake cabin on property my parents bought in the 1950's. I go skiing every winter with my brother. Presently I spend some time every week working on property we own on a bayou. My wife and I go to a gym and do aerobics and weights three times per week.

Now I know what some of you are thinking: That is fine for you if you like your hobbies but I love my job. Unfortunately, some people might need to work two jobs to get by. If you work long hours because you love your job and are married, please answer the following questions:

(1) Do you help your children with their homework and drive them to activities or do you leave that up to your spouse?
(2) If both spouses work, do you share the cooking and cleaning evenly?
(3) Do you and your spouse set aside time every week for just the two of you?
(4) How much time do you dedicate to a religious organization or charity?
(5) Do you go to the gym regularly or do other things for exercise?
(6) What activities have you taken up since your last graduation such as playing tennis, singing in a choir, painting a picture, hiking in the wilderness or volunteer work?

If you can work long hours without impacting your spouse and children, more power to you! If you do not have any hobbies, I hope you never have to retire.

After my retirement, I spent several years volunteering at the Covington Food Bank. There are studies that show that volunteers are happy people. The legal definition of a charity is an organization that does not make a profit. My definition of a charity is an organization run primarily by volunteers. When I worked at the Covington Food Bank only two people were paid money – a janitor and a part-time accountant we needed for taxes.

The people in charge were a retired couple who were far from wealthy. I believe that charities should be run by retired executives. Medical charities could be run by retired doctors. That is why I would never give money to the American Cancer Society or the Alzheimer's Association. According to the BBB Wise Giving Alliance (September, 2015) the chief executive for the American Cancer Society made $2,401,112 and the CEO of the Alzheimer's Association made $996,824. You would think these charities could find executives who had close family members with one of these illnesses who would work for a mere $300,000 per year.

From the BBB's website I took a random sample of 48 charities (September, 2015). Fifty percent (50 %) of the executives of the charities in my sample made over $187,000 per year and 25% made over $360,000. Only one of these 48 charities had a CEO, a minister, who took no money. I find it strange that people will not give a dollar to people begging for money on a street corner because they <u>might</u> have more money that it appears or they <u>might</u> spend their money on drugs or alcohol whereas they will give their money to a charity where it is <u>certain</u> that the executive makes over $500,000 per year.

Getting back to the subject of merit, there are other reasons for choosing an occupation. If you love your job, perhaps money is not so important. Perhaps a promotion would take you out of the position you most enjoy. Some occupations, such as physician, have few promotional opportunities.

The **Bureau of Labor Statistics** says that people born between 1957 and 1964 held an average of 11.7 jobs from ages 18 to 48. Certainly many of these job changes were not promotions. However, I would guess that professional people made fewer changes. Some possible reasons for a job change include:

(A) Finding less stressful work.
(B) Finding more interesting work.
(C) Finding more compatible management or coworkers.
(D) Allowing more time to be with your family.
(E) Allowing you to use other talents or to be more creative.
(F) Working in a place that better matches your philosophy and values.
(G) Living in a city more to your liking.

Note that everyone wants to work and live in a supportive environment. Everyone wants to maximize their talents and do what they do best or what they enjoy the most.

My purpose for writing this book is because I believe that merit truly is the forgotten dimension in choosing an occupation. The exception are entrepreneurs who want to blaze their own trail. They do not want to work for someone who will only slow them down or place obstacles in their way. When I became a psychologist, it never occurred to me that no one would ever want evidence that I could actually help others when I applied for a job. As I grew older and hopefully wiser, I came to realize that a Ph.D. in counseling is not sufficient to guarantee this person can truly improve one's life, especially the life of an addict. By contrast, after creating a computer program that saved the Army 500 man-hours per month, I no longer needed a degree to get a job in data processing.

Other Factors for Success in an Occupation

What traits relate to occupational success besides merit? Prestige, titles, certificates, networking, physical attractiveness, familiarity, social skills, and personal characteristic. Lastly, success can be a matter of timing and good luck.

Prestige

Our local newspaper once printed the names of the local high school valedictorians and what they intended to study in college. The most popular chosen occupation was medicine. Almost half of the female valedictorians chose something in the health services. Some valedictorians even claimed there was an undergraduate major called "pre-med".

Why do so many bright students want to be physicians? What do physicians do? As I mentioned previously, computers will make major inroads into diagnosis and treatment. Plus, some people conjecture that the majority of people in a doctor's waiting room will get better with or without treatment.

I don't want to give you the impression that I would not like a well-qualified physician for my doctor. With the exception of medical research, I just don't think we need the cream of the crop to go into medicine when the world has so many other difficult problems to solve.

For example, the United States has one of the highest rates of incarceration in the world. Do you know of any valedictorians going into the field of criminal justice? Prestige seems to be the answer as to why so many of the brightest students choose medicine. Do parents brag that their son or daughter is a criminologist or a sociologist?

Lawyer is another prestige occupation. Unlike physicians, some lawyers barely make a living while others make millions. Class action suits can make a lawyer rich. Lawyers get respect because law school is difficult. On the other hand, there are few jokes that make fun of physicians, except for psychiatrists, whereas we all know a lawyer joke – What do you have if ten lawyers are buried up to their necks in sand? Not enough sand!

Bankers were high on the prestige list years ago. Back in the old days we saw jobs as white collar and blue collar. White collar jobs such as banking were seen as prestigious. Today, only a few occupations require a suit and tie for the men. Usually these occupations involve sales. Today, people realize that many blue collar jobs pay well and are more likely to weather bad times.

Physicians still wear white coats. Even my eye doctor wears a white coat in case people with contagious eye diseases are roaming around the office. I have seen doctors show up at the gym in their scrubs. Evidently, they did not have time to change into their normal clothes.

Titles

Closely related to prestige are titles and certificates. One of the most popular titles is "doctor". If you go to college you can be "a bachelor of …", "a master of …", but only those with "a doctor of…" get a title. The word doctor comes from Latin meaning "to teach." At one time, any learned person who was qualified to teach a subject could be called doctor. Today the title "doctor" could indicate a physician, dentist, osteopath, a Ph.D. or even an honorary degree.

Let's consider the original definition for the title "doctor". A doctor is a person who is qualified to teach. Would that imply that a person who can do brilliant research but is a lousy teacher must give up his or her title? If you have never been to college but are an expert and teacher in a particular subject, can you use the doctor title or must there be an organization created to hand out these titles?

I suggest that if you are an expert in anything like fishing, poker, cooking pies, or television sitcoms you call yourself a doctor. You will find the title to be particularly helpful in getting good service in restaurants. If anyone asks where you received your degree, just say "it is an honorary degree".

When it comes to the title "doctor", I seem to be the ideal candidate to discuss it. I was the young "doctor" right out of college when I worked at a psychiatric hospital. I admit that I enjoyed the attention. As I matured, the following thoughts occurred to me. Do I deserve a title more than the following people: A wounded war veteran, a Nobel Prize winner, a single mother who works two jobs, or a man falsely imprisoned for 20 years?

Had I worked my way out of the ghetto to become my first family member to get a college degree by working nights and studying all of my spare time, perhaps I deserved a title. As it was, college was some of the most enjoyable years of my life. I played in the band, sang in the choir, and was a University of Minnesota gymnast.

While at the University of Texas working on my graduate degree, I was on a fellowship. I graded tests and gave lectures as a teaching assistant. I went with the ski club to Taos, New Mexico. I drove with friends to Mexico City. I drove my 1961 Austin Healey 3000 red convertible in Zilker Park at midnight with its hairpin turns. My roommate road with me once and never again. I still had time to volunteer at an institution for the retarded. I also volunteered at a facility where we talked down people on bad trips from taking LSD. I worked summers in Minnesota.

This was the 1960's. In Austin Texas every party and concert had the odor of marijuana. One of my roommates ran down the street half naked after taking LSD. I attended "happenings" and swam naked in the "camel's hole". I marched on the Texas State Capitol against the war in Viet Nam where marchers were gassed. I got people to sign the Hatfield-McGovern Amendment petition to end the war.

I needed two languages for my Ph.D. and was allowed to claim my self-taught "Fortran" as a language! If I could have only gotten them to give me credit for music as my second language I would have had a real story to tell. As it was, I could not survive a day in France but could pass a multiple choice test to get credit for French.

I not only enjoyed college, it prepared me for an interesting and well-paying job. I needed a title about as much as a million dollar movie star needs a little gold statue.

Keep in mind that the title "doctor" was first used in the days when we had kings and queens, dukes and duchesses, squires and knights. Without a title you were a mere peasant. At one time peasant meant farmer but quickly developed a less favorable connotation. So the real question is "if the United States decided that all men are created equal and we no longer have dukes and duchesses, why do we keep the doctor title?" There was a time when "mister" was a title. Now every male over the age of eighteen is a mister. A few people still use the terms "sir" and "madam".

The problem with titles is that they create a relationship of unequals. In economic theory, you and your physician are equals. You pay the physician according to the service provided. Without patients, physicians would make no money. Does your physician treat you with the same respect as the person who sells life insurance? Does your physician apologize for being behind schedule?

Another potential problem with a title "doctor" is that long after you have forgotten the facts you learned in college, you are likely to speak as if everything you say is the truth. I remember when I was at a seminar when the group had to choose from a selection of items to keep when stranded in the desert. A physician said we should not take a carton of beer as alcohol dehydrates you. Having worked with alcoholics I quickly responded "that is a myth". Any guesses who the group sided with? Thirty years later "An Institute of Medicine (IOM) expert panel concluded that most Americans get plenty of water not only from plain water but also from food, milk, juice, and even coffee, tea, and alcoholic beverages" (Tufts Health & Nutrition Letter, June 2017). Given that alcohol breaks down into carbon dioxide and water, I cannot understand why this myth persisted for so long

I know of more than one hospital that has problems with morale. I have a solution for improving hospital morale that requires no money. I suggest that the head of the hospital instruct everyone to be on a first name basis. Physicians could instruct staff and patients to refer to them by their first name or a nickname if desired. I predict that in six months morale will be improved. And yes, physicians can still tell the nurses what to do. Every business has people in charge and some people make more money than others.

Is there a place for titles? Certainly. The military needs titles and insignias because you always need to know who is in charge. This is particularly important when military personnel are frequently moved around.

Titles are important for people who represent official positions. The judge is "your honor" when on the bench. If he expects that title at the grocery store, he is mistaken. Likewise, when you are stopped for speeding you should refer to the person in uniform as "officer".

You can have a title even if it is not a part of your name. Titles are common in business. If your title starts with "Chief" you are important. Of course the president is at the top. Lowly people have no titles. If you are the Secretary of Defense, you are important. If you are an actual secretary, you must go by your name only. I was told that companies who want to save money have a lot of titles. Evidently a title can be a substitute for additional pay.

According to Miss Manners of the *Washington Post*, a congressman is "honorable" all of his life, and a senator is always a senator. I thought that people in government were supposed to be servants of the people. Since when do servants get titles?

Just as physicians have both prestige and money, so do congressmen. When our country was young it was suggested that congressmen serve without remuneration. The bad news is that this idea would limit congressmen to the wealthy. So how many poor people run for office these days? Without remuneration congressmen might be more likely to see themselves as public servants, and not someone trying to enhance his already substantial position. One of my pet peeves about congressmen is when they think their merit is reflected in the number of bills their name is on. Many of these bills represent the thinking of only one party or favor a lobby. I think a congressman has merit when he or she can work with someone from the opposite party to get legislation passed.

Certificates

Some occupations have various certificates or credentials. An accountant can become a Certified Public Accountant by passing a series of difficult tests. I would assume that CPA's generally make more money than accountants with only a degree in accounting. Teachers are often certified. As previously mentioned, counselors must pass a national test to become licensed.

Plumbers, electricians and carpenters need to have a license from the state. A license or certification provides proof of a certain level of expertise. It not only helps the pay level of the person certified but provides the warry recipient of the service that this person has the expertise necessary to do the job. When your toilet overflows you want someone you can be sure is capable of fixing it. Some of these same jobs have levels from apprentice to journeyman to master.

Obviously as your experience and credentials increase, so does your salary. Suppose you believe that you are one of the best master carpenters. Can you charge more for your services? Of course you can charge whatever you like but how does the public know you are worth it? If you are really exceptional, you might want to get on with a builder. Contractors should be decent judges of the work of tradesmen.

For better or worse, if you go into an occupation that has some type of certification, you can probably get a good estimate on the income you will make. Obviously, the big money is in eventually running your own business where you can hire the licensed or certified personnel.

The problem with certificates lies with the talented people who do not have them. You could have been making things out of wood since you were ten years old but how are going to sell your services as an adult if you do not have a state license? What kind of relationship are you going to have as an apprentice to someone who does inferior work to yours?

Diplomas and certificates look impressive on a wall. Some people have several. You can seldom go wrong with showing off an award. Various industries have their own awards. For example, a realtor might be a million dollar seller. The chef at an expensive restaurant might have won an award. Lowest on the totem pole are testimonials.

Networking (Who You Know)

For every book on choosing an occupation there are at least ten books on how to land a job. Most of these books talk about interviewing and resumes. They all mention the importance of networking. Not only do you let all of your friends know you are looking for a job but they recommend joining various groups such as LinkedIn. LinkedIn grew rapidly on the internet as a place to join yourself to others with similar job skills and ambitions. It features a profile page with a standardized format.

Every group you belong to such as a church, Kiwanis, Elks, etc. can be a source of contacts whether you are looking for a job or a mate. Of course many clubs and organizations are created for business. The Internet lists "The 8 most exclusive business clubs in Chicago". The *Harvard Business Review* recommends that business people join book clubs (Feb. 2016).

Networking is very important in rising to the top in some occupations. Obviously, this is especially important if you are part of a large company. It would be naïve to assume the people up the chain of command are aware of your abilities. Go-getters volunteer for extra work and various committees. Look to help out in the job you would like next. Your superiors need to know of your ambitions so you can be groomed for advancement.

The bigger the company or organization, the more important it is to know the right people. In the old days your parents got you into the right college (their Alma Mater) and whenever you came in contact with someone else from that college, you expected and usually received special treatment. The military can have a similar effect. Marine's respect other Marines.

Knowing the right people seems to be especially relevant for high level corporate positions. Former executives often become part of the Board of Directors. Some people believe the "Good Ol' Boy" system is responsible for the rapid growth of executive's salaries while the common worker's salary barely moves up. People with money might see each other at various charitable functions or at the country club.

Many books exist on how to succeed in business. They will more than likely recommend you find yourself a mentor who can groom you for your next position. Of course you have to be careful if you are dealing with a person you would like to replace!

You will need to be bold enough to find coworkers who will recommend you for a promotion or another position. Managers want to know more than your work achievements. They will want to know about your personal characteristics. Consequently, you will want your recommendations to come from someone who not only knows you well but someone who is respected. Always thank people who help you and do not be afraid to help others move up.

You need to not only let others know about your ambitions but to act like someone who is already in that position. Remember there is a chance that if you are too good in your present job, management may want to keep you there. Furthermore, if you are rejected for a job or position, politely find out why. You can learn from rejection.

Who you know at work is also related to job satisfaction. According to Gallup, job satisfaction is highest if you have a best friend at your place of work. Also related to job satisfaction is being respected and respecting senior leadership.

Anthropologists believe that humans are group animals that run in packs like dogs and wolves. Consequently, much of your perceived status is a function of the groups to which you belong. The status of any group you belong to will rub off on you. College students want to join the "in" fraternity or sorority. An ex-sailor always enjoys meeting another ex-sailor. If you went to an Ivy League school you will probably treat someone favorably from that same school. People take pride with living in a city with a winning football team, even if the players are from all over the country. We like people who are like us. Even nonconformists have merit with other nonconformists. Unfortunately, the reverse is true. We often do not favor people who belong to groups we are not a part of. An angel to one group of people might be the devil to another group.

Familiarity

Familiarity involves comfort with the known. People stick with familiarity to feel safe. Investors speak of familiarity bias. Gamblers will choose the horse they know over a strange horse with better odds. People like to stick with what they know. Familiar events are judged as more important. People overestimate the frequency of events with which they are familiar. People go with the familiar because it "feels right." Familiarity is one of the reasons that makes networking effective.

Some occupations use advertising to increase their familiarity. Personal injury lawyers spend a fortune on advertising. Advertising is powerful even when the ad in uninformative. Repetition keeps the product in your mind. Songs with a repetitious "hook" sell well.

Furthermore, any product (or person) can increase in value by association. A certain beer company knows that people like dogs and horses. Medical personnel like to tell you about special procedures they offer as if they only believed in public service advertisement. Financial advisors increase their familiarity by having radio shows. Is there any evidence that people with radio shows are tops in their fields (other than personal income)?

The bottom line is that the more familiarity you have within a company, the more you will be valued. Keep your boss (and even higher ups?) aware of everything you do of value. Greet coworkers in the hallways and let people know who you are.

Beauty/Physical Characteristics

What occupations provide an advantage to people who are physically attractive? I believe the answer is "just about all of them". In other words, if you were to send in two identical resumes with an attached picture of different applicants, who do you think would get the job? This technique was first used to show racial prejudice. According to the "Harvard Business Review" (October 11, 2017), white applicants received <u>36%</u> more interviews than blacks and 24% more interviews than Hispanics. A recent talk show host said that blacks were the most discriminated people. Wrong!

A study was done in Italy where 10,000 resumes were sent out with different pictures of the applicant. The average callback rate was 30%. For attractive women the rate was 54%, for unattractive women the rate was 7%, a difference of <u>47%</u>. For attractive men the callback rate was 47% and 26% for the unattractive men, a difference of 21% (*Business Insider*, September 13, 2013). Clearly, <u>unattractive women are the most discriminated people</u> in our society. Of course if you are an unattractive black woman, God help you! Ironically, including a photo greatly increases your chances of being viewed in LinkedIn. Of course if you are in the bottom 20% in attractiveness you may never get beyond the viewing stage.

Daniel Hammermesh wrote a book called "Beauty Pays" (2011). He says that an attractive man will make 13% more money than an unattractive man over the course of his career.

When I was young, you could get by as a singer by being a good singer. Those were the days with Mama Cass, Janice Joplin, Patsy Cline and Kate Smith. Opera even had a saying that it is not over until the fat lady sings. Surprisingly, it seemed like attractiveness was more important for male singers years ago. Frank Sinatra, Elvis Presley, and Ricky Nelson had the young ladies swooning.

During my lifetime I saw the female country singers getting more and more attractive. Only 2% of the world population is blond but you would never know it by looking at female country singers. I remember watching the country music awards in the 1990's. The first three female singers to perform were all stunningly beautiful. Then came an average looking woman I was not familiar with. I remember hollering to my wife in the other room – "You had better get in here. This woman must have a great voice."

I suggest that someone run the following study: Put two ladies singing on YouTube at the same time. Unknown to the viewers, both of the ladies will be lip-syncing the same song. One of these ladies will be young and attractive. The other lady will be middle-aged and plain looking. Then add up the "hits". There is no question that the young attractive woman will receive the most "hits"; I just do not know by how much.

Showmanship is a special type of beauty. Great showmanship can help propel a musician to the top. Elvis swayed his hips. Michael Jackson did a moon walk. Mick Jagger moves like a man on amphetamines. Kiss had recognizable outfits and tongues. Magicians rely on appearances, especially deceiving appearances. Optical illusions demonstrate how tenuous appearances can be.

Over the last ten years, television personalities have become more and more attractive. When I was growing up, only the weather girl was hired for her looks. Now whenever one of the major news programs brings in an expert, it is usually an attractive woman.

If you were to survey the CEO's of major companies, nearly all of them would be over the age of 50. Remember the days of Walter Cronkite and Huntley and Brinkley? Today, the television anchors have not only gotten more attractive but younger as well, and it is not just the women.

I can understand that attractive people help the ratings. I just wonder if the job application is honest in stating that the person must be young and attractive. There was a time when we had signs that said "colored". Getting rid of the signs did not mean discrimination was over. If I were a lawyer I would gladly take on cases of discrimination against people who are ugly. (Let's say overweight as no one wants to admit they are ugly.) Why? Because in all likelihood the job description does not say "must be attractive". If you believe you have good evidence that attractive people help your ratings, then why not include being "attractive" in the job description?

Hollywood clearly has more than its share of beautiful people. Movies and books often associate beauty with good and ugly with evil. Witches are not only evil, they are ugly. The Wizard of Oz had a good witch and a bad witch. It was easy to tell which witch was which by appearances. Devils and monsters are ugly. Angels and saints radiate beauty. This even translates into touch – furry creatures are good, slimy ones are not. Fortunately, there are a few ugly creatures that get our sympathy such as the Hunchback of Notre Dame or Shrek. However, no woman wants to kiss a frog unless she believes it will turn into a handsome prince.

In one sense, the movie industry is the least prejudice of all. Why? Because they are heavily influenced by the bottom line – money. Hollywood has plenty of money makers who are not young and beautiful. Helen Mirren is long past her prime but a producer would be crazy to pass her up for a movie role. She is a money maker. It may be helpful to be beautiful in Hollywood but at least everyone with talent and personality has a chance. Which brings me to Fox News.

Does Fox News even give ugly women a chance? Evidently, FOX News does not think older women are very smart either. Fox News had several women complain about sexual harassment. Supposedly, Fox News hires women who are highly intelligent. So how come a red flag was not raised when these women saw that nearly all of the women at Fox News were beautiful? Certainly the men were not all handsome. Their naivety is no excuse for sexual harassment but it makes you wonder what kind of a sheltered life did these women come from?

When was the last time you saw a pharmaceutical rep enter a doctor's office. If the rep was a woman, chances are she was beautiful. Are doctor's particularly shallow or are we all? Now that more and more physicians are women, we can expect fewer of these beauties. Advertising has always favored beautiful people. Almost by definition, people we like looking at are people who are beautiful. As I said earlier, advertising is unbiased. They will use whatever works. Budweiser exploits our fondness for animals. Some ads appeal to our sense of humor.

Being tall has an advantage for a man. The tallest presidential candidate received the popular vote in 67 percent of the elections. Probably broad shoulders is also a plus. In the United States, about 15 percent of men are over six feet tall. However, 58 percent of CEOs of Fortune 500 companies are over six feet.

Are we prejudice when it comes to good looks? The dictionary has more than one definitions of prejudice. One such definition is "any preconceived opinion or feeling, either favorable or unfavorable". In that case, we are all prejudiced. Some of these preconceived opinions come from evolution. Women with big breasts and wide hips made good mothers. Men who were big and strong made good hunters. Obviously, size no longer makes for a better CEO unless he intends to browbeat his employees.

Other characteristics we associate with beauty are high cheekbones, smooth skin and facial symmetry. Evolutionists believe that physical traits associated with good health translate into what we call beauty.

Some prejudices have changed over time. Slim people are not seen as desirable when food is scarce. Years ago the majority of gynecologists were men. Now (2018) only 17% are men. However, even today only 8% of urologists are women. Men do not have babies but don't all people pee?

With the help of the government, most companies do their best to avoid age discrimination. Never the less, applying for a job when you are over the age of 50 can be a daunting task and applying for a job when you are over the age of 60 is downright scary. Ironically, studies show that older people make for reliable workers. Older people have no sick children to attend to and probably go to bed early.

Furthermore, according to the Brookings Institution, there is no evidence that the performance of younger people is better (*The Impact of Population on Aging and Delayed Retirement on Workforce Productivity*, Gary Burtless, May 2013). Even in the use of technology, Ipsos Mori, a London-based market research firm, found that people 55 and up use on average 4.9 forms of technology per week compared to the overall average of 4.7 per week. Furthermore, compared with younger workers, older workers found using technology to be less stressful (cio.com).

I may have lost a job interview by appearing too young. One woman won a discrimination suit in part because her manager referred to her as "a kid". Obviously we have work laws regarding children so that they are not abused. For unknown reasons we believe you should not be president if you are under the age of 35. Teddy Roosevelt was our youngest president at age 42. The good news is that you can be a Supreme Court justice at any age. In fact you do not even need a high school education or be born in the United States. James Byrnes was a Supreme Court justice in the 1940's. He was also a congressman, senator, Secretary of State, and Governor of South Carolina. He quit school after the 7th grade!

The government does not allow discrimination on the basis of age, gender, religion or place of origin. Perhaps we should add ugly to the list. However, I don't think we will ever have an Association for the Advancement of Ugly People. Who would join? And can you see someone telling a judge in a discrimination case "Your honor, I am short, fat, and bald but not in a cute way. As you can plainly see, I am butt ugly".

Does your place of employment discriminate against ugly people? One third of our population is overweight. As a statistician it would be easy to show whether a company has a probability of less than 5% that their employees represent a random sample of the population in weight. When I worked for the Corps of Engineers under the Federal government, we had people of all shapes and sizes. A local oil company, that I will not name, clearly had less than their quota of the obese.

Oddly enough, I applied for a federal government position in Denver, Colorado. My mother lived there. When I called and asked why I did not receive an interview, the lady said it was because I did not live in Denver. I could understand this reasoning for a state government position but with the federal government? The federal government cannot discriminate on the basis of national origin but evidently if they do not like where you live in the United States, it is OK.

We have a federal law (Americans with Disabilities Act) that prohibits discrimination against people with **disabilities** who are qualified for a job. Places of employment need to be wheelchair friendly. Although there is not an exhaustive list of disabilities under the ADA, the regulations identify medical conditions that would easily be considered a disability within the meaning of the law (*Society for Human Resource Management*, November 6, 2017). These medical conditions are:

- Deafness.
- Blindness.
- Diabetes.
- Cancer.
- Epilepsy.
- Intellectual disabilities.
- Partial or completely missing limbs.

- Mobility impairments requiring the use of a wheel chair.
- Autism.
- Cerebral palsy.
- HIV infection.
- Multiple sclerosis.
- Muscular dystrophy.
- Major depressive disorder.
- Bipolar disorder.
- Post-traumatic stress disorder.
- Obsessive-compulsive disorder.
- Schizophrenia.

According to the 2010 Census, Adults age 21 to 64 with disabilities had median monthly earnings of $1,961 compared with $2,724 for those with no disability. The disabled had a 41.1% employment compared 79.1% employment for the non-disabled. If you have a disability, you definitely want to be in an occupation that rewards merit over appearances.

The appearance of being successful can be to your advantage in any occupation. Realtors drive around in expensive cars. Lawyers sit behind large and expensive desks. Back in the old days, one popular book was called "Dress for Success". Back then white collar workers actually had white collars with a suit and tie. Few jobs still call for suits. Oddly enough, a defendant in court will show up with a suit and tie, even if he had to go out and buy them. I worked with engineers where casual Friday had no meaning as jeans and tennis shoes were always in fashion.

I wrote a screenplay (unpublished) called "Teen Idol" where a corporation takes an average singer and makes him a star. One of their tricks was to film him in

Europe with screaming teenagers. This clip is used to further his career in the United States. However, the screaming teenagers in Europe were let in for free and told a movie was being made and that the more they screamed, the more likely they would be shown in the movie. In other words, one of the best ways to be famous in the arts is to convince people you are already famous. Furthermore, this teen idol was attractive and a good dancer which appeals to the younger audience.

Social Skills/Emotional IQ

We can probably agree that there is a certain unfairness about people rising to the top on their beauty or on who they know. However, most occupations rely on a certain amount of social skills. For better or worse, most of these skills are acquired from your environment as you grow up. Parents are the primary teachers of social skills. Parents say things such as "don't yell at your brother", "eat slowly", "treat your elders with respect", "smile more often", "don't slouch", and so forth. Children who grow up in impoverished environments lack more than just educational knowledge.

Emotional IQ involves recognizing your own emotions and the emotions of others, managing your emotions, motivating yourself and others, and demonstrating empathy and compassions. Of course using emotions to manipulate people is also a type of emotional IQ.

In my opinion, developing your emotional IQ after becoming an adult is difficult. Do you know of any adults who taught themselves to be nonjudgmental and

compassionate? Hopefully, religious exposure helps.
Social skills are usually learned by modeling others such as
our parents, siblings and peers. Things such as
understanding body language can be taught to some
extent.

Some of the tricks used by salespeople can be used
to endear yourself to others. Mimicking a person's body
language helps form a connection. Also, most people like
hearing their name. A good salesperson will identify with
one of your groups such as religion, political or even a
sports group. Also, people are proud of where they grew
up. If someone says "I grew up in Chicago" you might
respond with "Lake Michigan really looks great from the
Willis Tower". Most people are flattered if you ask for
their opinion. Everyone likes a good listener. Get a person
to talk about their hobbies and interests.

Years ago, finishing schools, sometimes called
"charm schools" focused on teaching social graces to
young girls whose parents were often in the upper classes.
Even the Cleavers send little Beaver to a dance class where
he will learn to be polite to the girls. "Final Touch", a
finishing school in the United States, teaches etiquette,
communication, image management, posture & presence
among other skills. Some programs are geared to young
professionals who want to learn how to deal with a variety
of personalities as well as make a good impression at job
interviews. If you grew up in a family of professionals, you
might have already picked up most of these necessary
social skills at home. If you grew up in a blue collar home
or was an only child, you might not be aware of the
unwritten expectations of your new professional job.

If you plan to travel abroad with your job, you will need to know how cultures vary as to what is expected. Some cultures are very formal while others are more casual. Sometimes, it is necessary to engage in small talk before discussing business. Even how close you stand to someone varies by culture. Can you be fashionably late or is being on time critical? Is formal dress (suit and tie?) necessary?

Just as I was rating occupations on merit, I could have been rating occupations on the importance of social skills. For example, a skilled surgeon can probably get by with few social skills. A high emotional IQ is a necessity for a salesperson. Also, social skills are a large part of being a good counselor. I wish that social skills were my forte. Fortunately I was able to hire someone who had these good social skills to be a counselor.

Personal Characteristics

Beside ability and beauty, there are many personal characteristics that are important in a job. Everybody has an idea of the personal characteristics that will help you succeed on the job. Here are three examples:

Attitude, Enthusiastic, Ethical, Goal Focused, Listener, Networked, Persistent, Self-Aware, Self-Confidence, and Self-Discipline (From *Timesunion*, Tom Denham, September 24, 2010).

Communication Skills, Honesty, Technical Competency, Work Ethic, Flexibility, Determination and Persistence, Ability to work in harmony with co-workers, Eager and Willing to Add to Their Knowledge Base and Skills, Problem

Solving Skills, and Loyalty (From *Employment Ontario*, May 23, 2015).

Passionate, Communication Skills, Goal Oriented, Organized and Detail Focused, Adaptable, Creative (From *Wasp*, Brian Sutter, March 21, 2016).

 I would add dependable, neat, thorough, grateful and a sense of humor.

      Honesty is important in most jobs. Honesty, or at least the appearance of honesty, is important in most every type of relationship. You need it in your marriage, on the job, and you look for it in the marketplace.

      The police have two suspects regarding a burglary that happened on Tuesday at 8:00 P.M. Each suspect is asked where they were at that time. Here are their answers:

Suspect A: "I remember I was on my computer checking my e-mail at about 7:30. I was probably on it for about twenty minutes. I was about to smoke a cigarette when I discovered I was out so I drove about a mile and a half to the convenience store at 7th and Elm. I bought a pack of Marlboros and some chips and headed home. I got back on my computer and checked out my Facebook page."

Suspect B: "I can't remember where I was last Tuesday evening. I was probably watching television as usual."

      Who is likely to be lying? According to the FBI, it would probably be suspect A. Liars tend to create elaborate stories. People telling the truth do not. There is an old saying that honest people do not need good memories. So ladies, if your husband comes home late and says "he stopped and got a beer with a friend" he is

124

probably telling the truth. However, if he has an elaborate story about how important it was for him to stay at work and finish a project comparing the costs involved between keeping the old accounting system or replacing it with a new financial package, you might want to call his boss the next morning.

Salesmen have learned a few tricks that are dishonest. A very common trick is the discount that never was. I used to drive by a jewelry store on my way to work. Every time I passed the store I noticed a sign that said 50% off. Considering the sign was always in the window it was clear the jewelry never sold for twice what they were offering it for. Never trust a discount unless you remember what the item used to sell for. Some stores mark everything up before their discount sale.

Another potentially dishonest trick is to make a person feel special. They will call you by your name and act like they are an old friend. They will let you in on a "secret" and give you a special deal. Salesmen also look for something about you they can connect with. Remember my sail boat story? To find a simple connection ask a person where they are from, what they do for a living, or how many children they have. After they give an answer it is your turn to respond with something that associates you with their answer. For example, if the person says "I have two boys and a girl" you respond with how many children you have. You might then ask about their ages or tell a funny story about one of your kids. Your response might be a true experience or a complete fabrication. The more you can both talk about your children, the more likely the person will see you as a friend. As a person opens up to you, you move in closer.

If you are dealing with a relatively naïve person you can make them feel special by telling the person that what I am doing is "just for you".

Being **dependable** is important in virtually all occupations. According to Bart McGuinn, a Human Resources director "If you ask any HR person they will tell you 80% of discharges are due to absenteeism and/or tardiness. The theme is "if you don't show up, failure follows." In my experience, musicians are not at the top for this measure. Do you have a job no one else can do? Does the company lose money if you are not on time or miss work altogether? Back in the old days, women who were liable to become pregnant had trouble getting work. For better or worse, more people today than ever do not take all of their vacation days.

Cooperating with other people is another trait important in almost all occupations. Many occupations rely on teamwork. If you are a part of a company that creates a product, chances are you will need to be a team player. You cannot build a product without plans. You cannot sell a product that doesn't exist. You cannot make money if your cost accounting is in error. A good exercise for a company is to ask "who in the company is missed the most when they are not at work?" Do not be surprised if most answer "the secretary". This is a person who works with everyone.

Just as there are personal characteristics that are important on the job, there are personal characteristics that will hinder your rise to the top. As a psychologist I have a long list of these personality traits:

Passive-aggressive or just aggressive

Narcistic, arrogant, egotistical

Impulsive, sociopathic

Perfectionist, obsessive-compulsive

Paranoid, distrustful

Reclusive, loner

Obstinate, set in your ways

Hysteroid, over emotional, drama queen

Depressed, lethargic

Cynical, pessimistic

Procrastinator

Prefabricator, liar, exaggerator

Kleptomaniac, thief

Hoarder

Unorganized, sloppy

Timing

Someone said "timing is everything." Success in any occupation could involve good timing. For example, you might choose a specialty that is expected to be big in the future. For example, you might go into engineering and specialize in solar power, hydrogen powered cars or the use of drones.

Timing could be a matter of choosing the right company in your profession or being in the right place at the right time when a supervisor retires. Of course being prepared for opportunities is necessary so that they do not pass you by.

Possibly I was in data processing at the right time and in psychology at the wrong time. Had I stayed two more years at Brainerd State Hospital I would have be grandfathered in as a licensed psychologist. Although counseling is not my forte, I could have at least did it part time in my specialty of the addictions.

Taylor Swift is a megastar today. Back in the early 1950's when the "Hit Parade" counted down to the number one hit, Taylor Swift would not have made the top ten. Why? Because back then middle aged people were the ones who bought records. I wonder what percent of Taylor Swift's paying audience is over the age of 40.

As I mentioned earlier, a publisher chose someone else's book over mine. I wonder what would have happened to my career if my book had been chosen. If it was successful I probably would have written a second book. Would having a published book helped me get a psychologist's job? Perhaps that was all I needed to be chosen on one of my second interviews.

Chance

All of us are subject to forces beyond our control. I know two beautiful and talented sopranos. In my opinion, they rank equally in talent. One of these ladies has performed at cities across the United States including New York, San Francisco, and Los Angeles. She sung in New Orleans with Placido Domingo. The other soprano has been mostly limited to local performances in New Orleans.

I have no idea as to why their achievements are not the same. However, I am sure I could find similar stories in just about every occupation. There could have been differences in their personalities or contacts that made a difference. However, it is possible that one major event can alter a person's whole life. Some people believe in the importance of preparation so that opportunities do not pass you by. Others believe in fate. You might even believe that you are given what you need. Perhaps, I needed to discover what it was like to be both the young psychologist who our hospital administrator called "brilliant" and to be the dishwasher that people talked down to. I did learn a lot about status from both perspectives. On the other hand, I just might have had bad luck. The point of this book is that you can decrease your chances of bad luck by entering an occupation where you rise to the top on your abilities.

Creating Merit

If you want a job where merit counts, you had better be a person with merit. There are many books to read on how to succeed including the habits and strategies of those who succeed. Let me add my two cents worth.

A recent idea is that you need 10,000 hours to be an expert. This idea is what I call "practice makes perfect on steroids". It is obviously only a half-truth. An example where this idea is pretty accurate is in athletics. I was a gymnast in college with a specialty on the high bar. The more you practice your routine, the better you get. Eventually your routine goes into body memory. Have you ever driven home from work and when you reach home you wonder if you drove through any stop signs? You have done this trip so often it is on auto-pilot. High bar involves split second decisions. Thinking slows you down. You need to practice enough to get on auto-pilot. It is possible that when athletes mention "flow", there are talking about the feelings of observing one's body on auto-pilot.

I love the Olympics and wondered why gymnast rarely fall and the best skaters fall more often than I would expect. Then I realized that skaters have too much time to think. As they are gaining speed for the quad jump I can almost hear them thinking "Picking up speed, getting close, here I go." My hypothesis can be tested. Look at skaters who do two difficult moves in a row. I predict that a skater is more likely to mess up the first move than the second move, given that the first move was successful. The skater has no time to think for the second move. It must be done from body memory.

What if you are a surgeon that repairs knees? Will 10,000 hours of surgery make you an expert? Not if your technique is wrong and your work does not last. In fact after years of bad knee surgery, it will be difficult for you to change your technique. A self-taught violinist can be a great amateur after 10,000 hours of practice but is unlikely to make the professional circuit if she learned to hold the bow incorrectly. In other words, 10,000 hours can make you an expert if you are learning the correct way to do something.

Can a person who is tone deaf be a professional musician with 10,000 hours of practice? It may be possible if you are a piano player or a drummer. On a piano, a G sharp and an A flat are the same note. A good violinist plays these notes slightly different. Perhaps you can learn perfect pitch. Let me give you another illustration. I weigh 125 pounds. How many hours of practice do I need to be an expert linebacker in football? Obviously, I could never become an expert linebacker.

People have merit in different ways. Some people are hardworking and dependable. Others are exacting and good with details. Some people are creative. They think out of the box. Other people are motivators and good with people. In the past, people worked on their weaknesses. The going philosophy today is to work on your strengths. For most tasks, a manager is not looking for someone who can do a little of everything. He wants someone with a specific skill. Being the best at one thing can make you in demand. Look at the medical profession. Specialists make more money than family doctors.

My strength is mathematics. I was born good at math. My dad excelled at math and both my brother and sister are good at it. Accordingly, I should have been in the right place when I worked as a statistician. However, I discovered psychology to be much more interesting to me. I am not a natural at psychology. I put a lot of effort into learning all I could about psychology. As I said earlier, I have 96 semester credits in psychology. I was excited to be able to create my own program for treating alcoholics. We were probably the first (and only?) to take recovering alcoholics to a bar. And yet it all made sense based on what I was taught in college. If an alcoholic can stay sober in a bar, he should be able to stay sober anywhere. Getting an award for what you are naturally good at does not compare to receiving an award for something you worked hard for.

There are plenty of general rules for success (demonstrating merit), and everyone needs to find what works best for them. I am a big believer in feedback. Don't do what looks good or feels right. Do what is most likely to produce the results you want. Behaviorists create charts to see if behaviors are moving in the desired direction. Who determines the desired direction? There is no one answer for that question. Hopefully, you know what you want. However, every society has written and unwritten rules. Moving in the right direction requires goals. Setting goals is a tricky subject. The *Federal Times* published an article of mine criticizing the VA hospitals for setting arbitrary goals (See Appendix 13).

In spite of my many classes in psychology, one of my greatest lessons came for W. Edward Deming, a physicist. He said "Don't change the person, change the environment that controls the actions of a person." (Not an exact quote) He made fun of companies that used posters to try and motivate people. If I were to ask social scientists how to lower crime, I expect most would talk about replacing punishment with rehabilitation. What would Deming say? I am guessing that he would have said "Get rid of cash." It is pretty hard to buy heroin with a credit card!

Merit in Relationships

Parents are known to praise children when they are good and scold them when they are bad. Unfortunately, many parents still think in terms of traits instead of actions. Child psychologists agree that you do not tell a child "you are bad" or "you are good". Instead they recommend that parents refer to specific actions which can be rated according to merit. For example, when one child hits another, the parent should not respond with "you are mean". Instead the parent should respond with "I do not like it when you hit your brother. If you do it again I will send you to your room." Likewise, the parent should indicate the merit of positive actions such as "I am so happy that you cleaned your room."

It is important than children learn early that people are not inherently good or bad, smart or dumb. Instead we all do things that can be seen as good or bad, smart or dumb. The child will learn the difference every time a parent refers to a specific action.

Unfortunately, we all have characteristics that rarely change. For example, some people will always be short and some tall. The problem is not a person's size but one's perception of it. Does a girl think that she is too tall and that boy's will not like her? Does a short boy have similar feelings? Whole children's books are written about accepting others who are different. In our society no one wants the label "fat". Too many pounds could be a potential medical problem. However, your weight could also make you the perfect lineman in pro football. Nevertheless, if you see a chart that relates obesity to diabetes, don't ignore it just because you do not want to feel bad. Negative feelings can compel you to action just as positive feelings can.

When I worked in a psychiatric hospital, I discovered that alcoholics would rather be called a drunk than crazy and schizophrenics would rather be called crazy than ugly. Part of a counselor's task is to help people discover or interpret what behaviors have merit and what beliefs need to change.

What does the concept of merit have in relationships? It depends on what we value. Some of the traits that we value include honesty, dependability, trustworthy, generosity, and compassion. Honesty is the foundation of a relationship. Every lie you tell will lower your merit. Every act of generosity and compassion will raise your merit. Think of your merit as a stock price. We like to think of our personal merit as rock solid but even events beyond our control can change how others see us. Smiles and "thank you" accumulate merit over time. Listening instead of talking will increase your merit.

Some personnel traits are harder to define than others. Most everyone says they like someone with a sense of humor. Men think the Three Stooges are funny. Women think that babies do funny things. Some people enjoy sarcasm while others see it as a type of hostility.

Treating people with respect will increase your merit. No one likes someone who acts superior. I know that from experience. Being a doormat will not help you either. Psychologists say "be assertive but not aggressive." Do not be afraid to defend yourselves and others.

You will always have disagreements with others. Some of the steps of conflict resolution are as follows:

(1) Use active listening (paraphrasing) to make sure you understand the conflict.
(2) Determine where you disagree and agree.
(3) See if the conflict can be rephrased in a different (more neutral) way.
(4) Does your conflict involve values or actions?

(5) Brainstorm as many ideas as possible withholding judgment.

(6) Look for common ground/compromise.

(7) Determine the responsibilities of each party.

(8) Work out a specific plan.

(9) Meet periodically to adjust dates or make changes.
   During the entire process be as nonjudgmental as you can. Clarify feelings as you go along. Use "I" messages. Praise any willingness to compromise. Obtain the services of a neutral party if you are not making progress.

The Golden Rule will keep your merit high. Instead of seeing yourself as a "good" person, I recommend counting your everyday actions as increasing or decreasing your merit.

Other Considerations

Variables that affect rising to the top include bias, supply and demand, and measurement considerations.

Bias

Bias, prejudice, discrimination and preference; these are all words with a similar denotation but not connotation. "Gentlemen Prefer Blonds" makes a good movie title. "Gentlemen are Prejudice against Brunettes" does not. In my opinion, the most common biases are not the usual prejudices we fight against. Our most common biases are being pro me and pro my group(s). We all know people who think everything they have is better. If I gave you ten photos and you were to rate them 1 to 10 in beauty, you would probably be in close agreement with the ratings of others. Now suppose I substituted your picture with one of the ten. Would you rate yourself lower, higher or about the same as everyone else rates you?

At Brainerd State Hospital we used significant others to evaluate our treatment. It is OK to get feedback from the patients, which we did, but patients have more than one reason to be biased. First, it is difficult for a lowly patient to criticize an important doctor. Second, some patients were hospitalized against their will, either by the courts or pushy relatives. They might want to give us a bad rating out of spite. Third, the most important reason for bias is what psychologists call "cognitive dissonance". Cognitive dissonance predicts that a person tries to line up their beliefs with their behaviors. In the simplest terms, if you are in a hospital you must be sick. If they are sent home you must be well. If a client spent over a year with a counselor and reported "no improvement" that would be equivalent to saying "I wasted my time and money". Sure, it is possible for a significant other to "see" progress because the patient has been released. However, it is also possible for the significant other to "see" no change if he believes psychiatry/counseling is bogus.

Psychologists speak about the importance of high self-esteem. At the same time, few people like someone who is conceited. What is the difference? People we like have high self-esteem. People we do not like are conceited. There are a lot of words in the English language that differ primarily on connotation. Psychologists tell us we should be spontaneous but not impulsive. If a woman jumps in bed with a stranger is she being spontaneous or impulsive? If that woman is you, clearly she is being spontaneous.

Most of us search the internet for answers to our questions. Clearly some of these web sites are biased. You might start by skipping any that says "ad". If I need medical information I start with the National Institute of Health. I also trust the Mayo Clinic, Cleveland Clinic and Johns Hopkins Hospital. I am a big believer in consensual validation. In other words, select several sources for some kind of agreement. This is not as easy as it sounds as many sources get their information from the same place. That is why so many people believe that alcohol dehydrates you. The internet has several articles explaining exactly how alcohol dehydrates you. Scientists often parrot other scientists but try to find a study where the subjects' blood and urine are actually tested from those who drank alcohol against those who drank water. Try to find an article that explains why some regular beer drinkers can drink a six pack without peeing. Note: I am not saying that alcohol hydrates you as well as water. I am only saying it does not dehydrate you, especially if you are a regular drinker. Furthermore, it is the intermediate stage in the breakdown of alcohol that can ruin your liver.

The internet is not a research journal. There are few sites that summarize a research study, let alone does a summary of related research know as a meta-analysis. I get lots of advice on healthy eating from friends. That is why I decided I would stick to the advice given in *Tufts Health & Nutrition Letter*. Their articles are primarily a summary of research. It is easy for me to believe that too much saturated fat can increase your risk of heart disease by 18% when it is based on following 73,000 females and 42,000 males for 28 years (May 2017).

I am one of the few people that knows paraprofessionals make the best counselors. You cannot find this on the internet because the studies were done in the 1980's. Evidently, counseling psychologists quit comparing paraprofessionals with professionals after discovering that nobody cares. I expect that in the future some graduate student will compare licensed professional counselors with life coaches and the debate will begin all over again. Hopefully someone will find my e-book that explains it all.

My biggest complaint of various sources of healthy eating is that they will point out a food containing an undesirable element such as a known carcinogen but will not tell you how much it contains or what the accepted level for this element is. I had my house in the bayou tested for mold. I had <u>seven</u> types of mold. If I had not had the mold tested outside of my house as a control, I would not have known that five of the seven molds were just as high outside of my house as inside. Fortunately, the other two were at levels too low to be of concern.

Even scientific journal articles cannot be fully trusted. Pharmaceutical companies do the research on their own drugs or contract out to those they trust (as in trust to want more money for future research?). Furthermore, studies that show negative results are less likely to be published. Periodically, statisticians, as a hobby, like to point out the statistical and methodological flaws in research articles.

The use of **comparisons** can make something look better or worse. When you are selling a Buick you compare it with a smaller automobile. You do not compare it with a Lexus or Mercedes.

When I was working for Waterborne Commerce I wanted to replace a man who was retiring from another office. This man had done little to modernize his office. I could have looked good by comparison in as little as one year. On the other hand I did not want to replace my boss should he retire. He was a wiz at finances; a weakness of mine. My motto is "learn from the best but replace the worst." As an example, be an assistant coach for a winning team and become the new coach of a losing team.

One of my specialties was setting up interviews for job applicants at WCSC. In my experience hardly anyone considers the talent or lack of it in who they might be replacing. Comparisons are critical to looking good. Why do we revere President Lincoln? Could it be in part because he was a president during difficult times? Would we think he was a great president if he were president during good economic times when the country was unified? The same goes for Franklin Delano Roosevelt.

Comparisons are relevant in our personal lives. Women are attracted to widowers but she faces the possibility of looking bad by comparison to a dead wife who has now become a saint. Find a man who divorced a real loser and you can look good by comparison.

There is an exception to the comparison rule and that is the **group rule**. You look better if you belong to "good" groups and you look worse if you belong to "bad" groups. This conflict of rules can be very tricky in personal relationships. For example, if you go out to a bar with a single friend, an attractive friend can make you appear more unattractive. However, if you go to a bar with a group of friends, good looking friends will make you appear more attractive. The status of any group you belong to will rub off on you. College students want to join the "in" fraternity or sorority. People with a winning football team feel better about themselves even if they do not personally know anyone on the team.

Often it is clear which groups have the most status and prestige. Being a graduate of an Ivy League school can help you get a job even if you barely passed. Having a celebrity as an acquaintance, even a minor one, can help your appearance. This could be a local newscaster, politician, musician, author, painter, sports figure, etc. Logically, knowing someone important has absolutely no relevance to your abilities or personal traits. Humans are pack animals. We are defined by our groups – the church we belong to, the job we work at, the political party we support, the clubs we attend. Some people will go as far as cultivating relationships with important people such as their doctor so they can name drop.

Many of the groups we belong to only make us look better to other members of the group. For example, being a republican will make you look better to other republicans but not to democrats. Likewise, being in the Sierra Club will make you look good to those in the "green" movement. Even rebels are seldom loners. Rebels simply belong to small groups. If you love the gothic look you will appear more desirable to the small number of people in this group.

Supply and Demand

Probably the most confounding variable to the metric dimension is supply and demand. Evidently there exist many personal injury lawyers. They spend a lot of money advertising their services. I wished that physicians advertised their prices. Perhaps they do not need to list their prices because they have all of the patients they desire. As of June 5, 2017, "HealthGrades" lists 72,798 Family Medicine physicians that received grades (stars) from 1 to 5. Of those physicians, only 3,405 (4.5%) list themselves as available. For what it is worth, of the available physicians, 42.2% are women. 50.9% of these women received 5 stars and 33.3% of these women received 1 star. However, looking at every rated physician, men and women score about the same.

Perhaps I had to compete with a lot of psychologists for jobs but competed with very few people in data processing. However, one could argue that in a very competitive field it is especially important that you separate yourself from the pack with exceptional ability. If you are in an occupation with a lot of competition but little interest in merit, your odds of being selected go down considerably. On the other hand, if you need a plumber and you need him now, you will take the next one available.

For some occupations, supply and demand varies considerable over time. I know this is true for nurses and engineers. When the job market is tight, it seems like many people go back to college to get their MBA degree which reduces its value. The trades of electrician, plumber and carpenter always seem to be in demand. Anything related to technology is probably a good choice. Also, a job that relates to our aging population has got to be a winner.

It is hard to predict the demand for creative fields. What sells for a writer? Is it better to write fiction or nonfiction? Can you make a living writing magazine articles? How many musicians would like to play for a symphony orchestra? Is a bassoonist in greater demand than a violinist?

In any case, a young person choosing an occupation needs to consider supply and demand. This might take a bit of research for unusual occupations. I have heard it said that it is harder to become a veterinarian than a physician. Physicians only have to deal with one species.

Measurement Considerations

All sports involve a principle statisticians call minimum variation. For example, shooting a gun at a target might have a rating very close to a 10. It cannot be a perfect 10 because if the gun were put in a vice so that it could not move, the bullets would still show some variation around the target. The better the gun and the ammunition, the smaller the variation.

Interestingly, **shooting free throws in basketball is probably as close to a 10** as you can get on the merit scale. Why? Because the hoop is larger than the basketball. You can shoot a basketball toward the center of the hoop and be off by as much as 8 inches and still make the basket. Plus the shooter can take his time to shoot and there is no interference from any competitor. You can be five feet tall and still be the best at free throws.

Shooting free throws brings up another consideration by statisticians – How accurate is a sport's statistic. Let's suppose you shot 7 out of 10 free throws. You make free throws 70% of the time. Because you only threw 10 free throws, this 70% statistic may not be accurate. However, if you made 70 out of 100 free throws, this 70% statistic would be very accurate. Obviously, as the number of throws gets higher, your free throw statistic approaches the "true" value.

Don't make the mistake of thinking that 20 free throws gives you twice as good reliability as 10 throws. Statisticians will tell you that you can predict the winner of an election quite accurately with a sample of only a few thousand people, given that these people make up a good representation of the voting population. You will reach a point sooner than most people realize where doubling your sample improves your prediction only slightly.

The sports of soccer and hockey are low scoring. Clearly a lot of games need to be played in order to judge the quality of the teams and individual players. As previously mentioned, baseball is a sport highly dependent on the pitchers. You might be the best right fielder ever but it will be hard for you to get recognition playing on a team with poor pitching and batting.

If you want to be in a sport or occupation where merit counts, you want to choose an endeavor where the measures of success have both reliability and validity. Reliability implies that the measures used are consistent, that is, if you were to repeat the measure you would score about the same. Fortunately, statisticians are able to measure reliability using correlation. Two judges could give ten skaters scores and a reliability coefficient could be determined. Perfect agreement would be a correlation of 1.00. No relationship would be near zero. A negative relationship would imply that either they are immensely biased or are basing their judgment on different things.

Statisticians even have a way of determining if two measures are significantly different. Clearly what is significant depends on the number of measurements. If you threw a coin in the air 10 times and got 8 "heads" you would not be surprised. However, if you threw a coin in the air 100 times and got 80 "heads" you would think the coin was improperly weighted. The bottom line is that <u>if you are in an occupation where there are no ways to accurately and consistently measuring success, you are in an occupation where merit does not count.</u>

Validity implies that the measurement actually measures what it intends to measure. The original intention of the IQ test was to determine who could and could not benefit from a formal education. Even today there is a good correlation between IQ and success in college.   On the other hand, IQ may not be a good measure of "innate" ability.

Unfortunately, in my opinion, there is something called "face validity". This means that the measure "looks good". The exam to become a licensed counselor has face validity. To the best of my knowledge there are no studies that show that high scorers make the best counselors. Even with an exam as comprehensive and as serious as the test to get into medical school (MCAT), has anyone shown that high scorers make the best physicians? MCAT scores, however, are related to making it through medical school. Conscientiousness is also related to making it through medical school (Lievers, J. Applied Psychology, Nov. 2009).

Another question I alluded to earlier is that if you have a valid and reliable measure of ability, why do you insist on a college education? I expect that no one has ever asked an athlete trying out for the Olympics if they received an "A" in a physical education class. If you are a sprinter and can do the 100 meters in under 10 seconds you could have dropped out of school in the eighth grade. Likewise, why would anyone care about the formal education of anyone who can pass the four rigorous CPA exams? In earlier times, you only needed to pass the bar exams to become a lawyer.

It stands to reason that the most critical jobs require rigid qualifications. You want a doctor, a lawyer and a tax consultant to know what they are doing. Your life and livelihood could depend on them. So what job is probably the most critical? Might it be the president of the United States? Just being Commander in Chief makes this job a matter of life and death. What are the qualifications? Must they show passing grades in political science, geography and history? The qualifications to be president of the United States is to be a natural-born U.S. citizen and be over 35 years old. Wow! That really screens out the incompetent! Would you believe that the African country of Angola at least requires a solid educational background? On the positive side, in the United States, even a convicted felon can be president (or ex-president).

Let us look at some of the qualifications of U.S. presidents. Eleven presidents had no college degree.

Abraham Lincoln only had about 2 years of formal education. Harry Truman had only a high school education. Donald Trump, as well as four others including two generals, never held any previous political office. Twenty-six presidents were lawyers. Don't lawyers thrive more on confrontation than cooperation? I would like to see a president that stresses planning and cooperation more than problem solving and intimidation (See Appendix 14). I am not even going to attempt to rate politicians on the merit scale. If I wanted to run for public office, I think I would major in theater.

If you think I am advocating for more standards for the presidency, I am actually advocating for less standards for many other occupations. President Lincoln did a pretty good job with so little formal education. Given the Internet, formal education seems to be less and less important as a requirement for most jobs. I believe the states should set up testing centers similar to those they have for qualifying for a driver's license. A computer can generate a test on the fly from several hundred test questions of known difficulty. Passing a series of tests for a particular subject matter such as algebra should qualify you for credit good at any state college or university. Obviously, some subjects require you to attend class such as chemistry lab and possibly a discussion group. Presently, colleges do more with the internet and computerized learning than ever but offer little in the way of reduced tuition. I am not advocating that the government provide free education as some countries do. I am advocating that we make use of the considerable savings involved in learning from a DVD or over the internet. My former university asks for my money because they are doing great things. I will gladly send money when

I hear that they have razed a few buildings because students are learning over the internet.

Several years ago psychologists decided to create a Doctor of Psychology degree so a person no longer needed to pass statistics to do counseling. Given that counseling psychologists with statistics do no pre and post testing, a class in statistics is hardly necessary. I actually agree that a counselor does not need to know statistics. I believe the state licensing boards for psychologists should do the pre and post testing for clients of counseling. As I previously mentioned, at a minimum the state licensing boards should create a website where clients can do counselor evaluations. They could actually do publishable research in counseling by including temporary questions. For example, do clients do better with someone of the same sex? I believe that a counselor would achieved better results by speaking with the significant other of a client. I could be wrong but the research would be easy to do from a website. The state licensing board could require all counselors to notify their clients of the website and encourage them to respond.

My specialties as a psychologist were alcohol and drug dependency and program evaluation. The recent opioid crisis has convinced people that drug dependency requires treatment instead of jail. Just as I cannot recommend a counselor, I cannot recommend a treatment center for addiction. People who are depressed, anxious, or have relationship problems enter counseling at a low point. Consequently, most will get better with or without treatment. The success of counseling needs to be compared with a suitable control group. Unfortunately, addicts seem to be the exception. Addicts seldom get better without help. The gold standard for measuring the success of a program for treating addiction is the percent of clients who go one year without relapse. I cannot recommend any addiction treatment center that does not routinely collect this data. Neither should any government fund any such center. Would you buy stock in a company that had no quarterly report?

During a health fair I asked someone representing a treatment center for alcoholism what was their success rate. He replied "80% for those that stick with the program". I spoke at a VA hospital and said I had a success rate of 100% for those who stick to the program. They thought I was kidding. I said "no, it's true". I sit across the table from a client and tell them "don't drink". Everyone who follows my program gets better. I might add that if treatment centers truly had an 80% success rate, they would be up for a Noble prize. People make up these figures at health fairs as well as ads in the media. At Brainerd State Hospital where I worked, nearly one-third of our admissions to our chemical dependency program where readmissions. You need to do serious work to find out who died, who moved out of state, and who is in another treatment facility.

If you want to be in an occupation where ability counts, you need one that has metrics beyond the ratings of customers. For example, a restaurant might get high customer ratings and get closed down by the health department for unsanitary conditions. Customer ratings are great for telling you about people skills. Friendly, helpful workers get good ratings. Your dentist might be the nicest person in the world and do unnecessary work on your teeth.

The importance of people skills varies from job to job. If you are a salesperson, people skills are at the top of the list. If you are a teacher, the ability to motivate a child is important but so are gains on standardized tests. I personally can tolerate a physician who is arrogant and abrasive as long as I am convinced she can be a life saver.

If an occupation does not have true metrics such as quarterly sales, I would consider peer ratings. Why doesn't someone create a company that pays workers/companies to rate each other? In my opinion, this would be a better gauge than customer ratings. I have discovered that nurses are a reliable source for rating physicians. In New Orleans, "City Business" selects the best companies to work for based on employee ratings.

Most employees are rated by their supervisors. These ratings are critical in moving up in a government job. Obviously, it is important that the criteria for the ratings represent true measures of job performance. This task of creating valid measures can be very difficult when the job does not have well established outputs.

Conclusions

What are the primary lessons I learned that I tried to convey to you in this book? This is a test of your retention although it is possible that your score reflects the ability of your teacher.

One, the obvious answer is that if you like being rewarded for your skills and talent, you might consider choosing an occupation high on the merit scale. Consider any occupation that lets you work for yourself. Otherwise, choose an occupation with clear standards and reliable measurements of success.

Two, people skills count for a lot at work and in everyday life. As a reward for those of you who made it this far, I am going to give you some advice for your children, grandchildren or anyone between the ages of 6 and 16. Given the choice of supplementing their academic studies with either music lessons or participation in a team sport, choose the team sport. Why? Music is a great hobby. I should know. However, you can learn to play an instrument at any time in your life. Many a person took up the piano after retirement. Trying to learn people skills as an adult is difficult. I can talk forever on "intellectual" topics but when it comes to small talk, I am done after asking about the kids and commenting on the weather. As I have said earlier, I can teach counseling. I just shouldn't do it.

Team sports teach children how to be part of a group. Pack animals survive by strength in numbers. Although individuals may have different functions, they all promote the welfare of the group. No matter how many superstars are on a baseball team, they will never reach the top without group spirit. People who have played on a championship team can describe what this means better than I. The best I can say is it means putting the interests of the team ahead of your own. It means helping your teammates whenever possible. There is also an encouragement/optimism that infects a winning group; a "can do" attitude. The military provides a similar environment.

Before a child is ready for team sports, there is preschool. Preschool through kindergarten is for exploring the world with all of your senses. Youngsters develop physical coordination. They also learn how to relate to other children.

Some parents still insist on teaching their children to read when they are four years old. The other children will catch up to them in the third or fourth grade. The reason that parents continue to do this is because they, themselves, are brighter than most people. Consequently, they do not realize that their children would be exceptional in the third and fourth grade without early learning. High school students in Finland excel on standardized tests. They do not start academics until they are seven years old.

A child's brain is primed for learning a language from about age 2 through age 5 or 6. So instead of teaching your child reading, writing and arithmetic, teach the child a second language. It is no longer believed that learning two languages at once will confuse a child. Music involves sounds, just like language. Although the "Mozart effect" has been largely discredited, children introduced to music at an early age (before they are old enough for team sports) increases their chances of developing perfect pitch. Studies show that music is good for the brain at any age and can be relaxing and an aid to sleep.

Three, the cost of an education is cheaper than ever. I groan whenever anyone talks about how much education costs. What they mean is that college costs a lot of money. I can learn a language over the internet for free through a program sponsored by my local library. Learning can be fun. Want to learn about World War II? You don't need a college course. Come to the World War II museum in New Orleans and spend a week there. The

Khan Academy offers free classes. Even major colleges like Yale, Harvard and MIT offer free courses over the internet. Hopefully, some day they may give you transferable credit for these.

Just as Amazon has made buying easier, the internet has made learning easier. Soon the big colleges will go the way of Sears, Macy's and other big department stores. Colleges will be fewer and those that remain will offer classes over the internet at a reduced rate.

Keep in mind that no one knows the monetary value of a college education. I suggested to the Bill and Melinda Gates foundation they do the following study:

1. Give each of 200 high school graduates $80,000.
2. Randomly select 100 of those who can only spend this money on a college education.
3. The other 100 can spend this money away they want but cannot attend college.
4. Follow the 200 people for several years (20?) and compare their incomes.

I for one have no idea what the results might be but I would like to know.

I feel confident talking about education. I spent eight years in college. I taught at college. I spent three years evaluating educational programs. I was lucky. I went to college when tuition was relatively cheap. The University of Texas had oil money. Their tuition for an out-of-state student was about the same as an in-state student in Minnesota. Universities are still great places to do research. Unfortunately, researchers are not always the best teachers.

Ironically, we have taken a step backwards in some respects. Back in the 1800's students of various ages were in a classroom together. Not only did this allow a student to go at her own pace but it allowed for the older students to help the younger ones. As previously mentioned, we also had finishing schools that taught social graces. I certainly could have used one of those.

Four, companies need to develop their own criteria for prospective employees. (I didn't really talk much about this earlier so we won't count this one on the test.) Companies need to get rid of their degree requirements and create their own tests to measure what they are looking for in an employee. Lincoln made a pretty good president with little formal education.

Some companies already do this. I remember looking at an employment test from Google several years ago. You not only needed to be brilliant to pass this test, you needed to be creative. Can you create a sorting algorithm and a haiku? I already mentioned how the federal government would not let me give a test in basic statistics for hiring a statistician. Whereas the federal government required a degree, a got a summer job with the state of Minnesota by getting a perfect score on the research analyst test.

I know you are tired of me bragging about my test scores but I am not really that smart. I do well on tests because I grew up on games and therefore have no test anxiety. For better or worse, I never mentioned my Graduate Record Exam scores when applying for a job. I thought my accomplishments were sufficient. Furthermore, my wife, having more people skills than I, made it clear to me to never tell anyone my scores on the

Graduate Record Exam. (If this book sells like my other book, my secret is safe.) In fact, I have been a member of the New Orleans Concert Band for over twenty years and not a single band member knows I have a Ph.D. I feel I need to emphasize my intellectual skills as a lesson in how much more important it can be to have people skills (with the exception of a small number of technical jobs).

There are three basic advantages for a company to develop their own tests. First, you know what the job requires. I used to ask prospective employees if they were better at speed or accuracy. About 80% said accuracy. As it turns out, we put out a publication on a yearly basis. Our biggest complaint was that we were late. Without this question, we would continue to be late.

Second, your own test allows you to look for traits unrelated to a formal education. If the job requires a team player you need to find out about this person's experiences with teams. Does the job involve travel? Does the job require a lot of overtime? Does the job require creativity? Developing the right questions is tricky. If you advertise the job as involving travel you can bet that all of your applicants will say they like to travel. However, asking a job applicant "where is the farthest you have ever been from home?" might eliminate the home bodies who desperately need work.

Third, as I mentioned previously, feedback is the only way to get better. Your first try at creating a company test might be a flop. However, over time you can see how your better employees answered your test questions and make appropriate changes. You can still look at transcripts if you like. If you do, you will need to verify as to whether the people with the best grades made the best employees.

Feedback not only helps you get better (increase your merit), you need norms or standards. I could improve as an individual counselor by doing follow-up on former clients, but I could improve even more by comparing my scores to other counselors and finding out how I differ from the best of them.

Feedback should rely on more than surveys and opinions. For example, readmission rates is a stronger metric than opinions for measuring the success of a hospital program. Physicists differ as to whether string theory or loop quantum gravity is the best "theory of everything" but the hard sciences rarely resort to opinion to settle differences.

<u>Five</u>, we need to treat everyone and all occupations with respect. We are all prejudiced. We like people who are beautiful, rich and smart.

Let's start with beauty first. I do not believe it is shallow to favor beautiful people. In fact, as mentioned earlier, I believe it is in our genetic makeup. The good news is that we can all do something to enhance our physical image. Looking good is a billion dollar industry from the way we dress, our personal grooming, perfumes and colognes, and diet and exercise. Cosmetic surgery is more popular than ever. Ladies, if you like the attention of men, I see nothing wrong with breast enhancement. Balding men can go for hair restoration.

Looking good at work can be as simple as a neat desk with a family photo. A wall with a diploma, certificates and awards won't hurt any as long as you do not draw too much attention to them. A friendly smile adds beauty to anyone.

If you want to know if this is a good place to work or a good place to live, never ask an attractive young lady. In my opinion, attractive young women are treated the best. Consequently, if they say this a good place to work it means nothing. Ask someone old and unattractive. They will tell you the truth. I think it would be a good idea if every attractive young lady spent a few days in a fat suit with makeup to look ugly. I think it would be a life changer.

Speaking of appearances, most people are prejudiced against the mentally ill. Fortunately, this is changing for the better. At Brainerd State Hospital I taught patients to "walk proudly." People can be taught to change their body language. I know it is difficult. I still have to remind myself of eye contact when talking to others. This could be a whole new specialty (within cosmetology?), analyzing a person's body language and working on corrections.

Enough has already been said by others about our prejudices based on sex and skin color. As I am writing this book, the United States has a major problem with opioid addiction. If I were a black person I would be furious. When black people took opioids it was a crime. Now that white people are hooked it is a medical condition.

Are we prejudice toward rich people? Definitely. You might despise them or cozy up to them but few people treat them like everyone else. Most people would like to be rich. There is an old saying "I've been poor and I've been rich and rich is better." Sure there are problems with being rich. If you won 50 million dollars in the lottery you would have to move and change your name. Every friend and distant relative would contact you. Every charity would put you on their list. Every time you went out to dinner with others, they would expect you to pay the bill.

Men especially want to be rich. They believe that's their ticket to dating beautiful women. Have you ever seen an ugly doctor who could not get a date? I cannot imagine what it is like being a movie star – rich, famous and attractive.

One of the advantages of being rich is that rich people make the laws. Considering it is rich people that run the companies and hire the workers, why not give them a tax break for hiring people, not a tax advantage simply because they are rich? I have already mentioned how landlords and homeowners get the tax breaks and renters get squat. In the past, a large gap between the "haves" and "have nots" led to revolutions. Hopefully, the revolution in the United States will be political only.

We will always have people who are beautiful and people that are rich. However, when it comes to titles, certificates and awards, this is something completely under our control. Our constitution states the "all men are created equal". This is usually interpreted as equal in rights. Every Sunday my church has us recite a prayer that says we should treat all people with dignity and respect.

Titles and awards tell us who the best people are, or as George Orwell once said "All animals are equal, but some animals are more equal than others." Of course we all know that some people are more talented than others but do we need to be constantly reminded of it? This is especially true in the entertainment field. Can't we at least televise the handing out of Nobel prizes?

I suggest we reward people with money. If you are a top tennis player or golfer you are already rewarded with cash. (OK, you might also get a green jacket.) There are three good reasons for rewarding people with money. One, most people would prefer money to a plaque. Two, people who are movie stars, top athletes and noted scientists already have a lot of money. They can pass this award money on to their favorite charity. If I have to listen to the already rich and famous actresses and singers pretend that their third award is surely the best one they ever received at least I will know it is for a good cause.

Let's talk about titles. We no longer have dukes, squires and noblemen. I say it is time to rid ourselves of the title "doctor". Just as my background makes me ideal for criticizing a college education, I am also eminently qualified to advocate getting rid of the title "doctor". At Brainerd State Hospital I had the title "doctor". I know how people treated me. Would you believe that a physician gave me a "professional discount" just because of my title? I also know how people treat you when you are sweeping floors or washing dishes. When a counselor uses the title "doctor" he now has "patients". Without the title a counselor has "clients". Clients have power. They pay the bills of professionals. Patients are helpless. They need to be taken care of.

If you are a counselor, I believe there is another reason for getting rid of the title – people are less honest with you. This is not a proven fact but is one of the explanations as to why paraprofessionals make better counselors than professionals. Addicts feel more comfortable getting help from former addicts. They feel better understood. I would add that sometimes a former addict can make a bad counselor by assuming too much in common. If you drank or took drugs because of peer pressure, would you know how to deal with someone who drank or took drugs because of high anxiety? Keep in mind that the addicted all look alike when they hit rock bottom. As previously mentioned, chemical dependency was one of my specialties as a psychologist. I not only studied the literature, I had a father die from it at the age of 57.

In any case, I would like to see a study comparing the honesty of clients dealing with someone with the doctor title versus someone without it. I would also like a study to see if people who grew up in troubled homes make better counselors than people who grew up in stable homes.

The problem with physicians being called "doctors" is a little trickier. Perhaps a patient is more likely to follow the advice of someone with a title. On the other hand, if you disagree with your physician, maybe the "doctor" title is getting in your way. How many people take medicine that does not work because their doctor prescribed it? The elderly, especially, seem to be on too many medications. For some people the title "doctor" is clearly intimidating. This problem is not entirely the physician's fault. Most physicians would like an honest assessment of how well you are doing. Medicines often need to be adjusted for dosage. Perhaps your prescription needs to be switched to a different one of dropped altogether. I am hoping that someday a hospital with morale problems will take my advice and try going six months with everyone on a first name basis. After a rough start I think that morale would go up, but I could be wrong.

If you tell me that physicians need a title because they save lives, they are not the only ones who save lives. I live in a city with a high murder rate. I live in a state that incarcerates more people per population that anywhere in the world. I would bet my Ph.D. in psychology that if for the past 50 years only criminologists were given the title "doctor", crime would be down. Remember the television program called "Numbers"? They had physicists solving crimes. I always thought that police departments need to use drones like our military does. Drones could prevent high speed car chases. Drones are not afraid to go into poor neighborhoods at night. Drones do not shoot first out of fear. We need more (assuming we have any) valedictorians going into this field. However, if there is any group most deserving of a title, it would be injured war veterans. I wouldn't mind if they got the best tables at restaurants.

I believe the biggest problem with the title "doctor" is that the title has a great influence on which students choose to become physicians. Unfortunately, this title also influences the parents who would like to brag about their children. Are these students really interested in medicine? I suggest the following study: Follow the people who applied to medical school(s) and were not accepted. If they truly love medicine, a large number or these people will have become nurses, physician assistants and various medical technicians. If you find more lawyers, MBA's, and entrepreneurs among them it would appear that money and prestige is more to their liking. Of course I am talking about the men. I am not sure about the women.

Clearly I am prejudiced against counseling psychologists and physicians. I cannot recommend a counselor because counselors maintain no data to demonstrate effectiveness. Neither can I recommend a treatment center for addiction. Over the last 50 years I have contacted numerous treatment centers. I have yet to find one that routinely collects follow-up data. Hazelden, at least, has done a one-time study. The gold standard for addiction treatment success is to be sober/clean for one year after treatment. I believe that treatment centers should not receive accreditation without this data. Let me make this clear. I do not require a treatment center to show effectiveness to be accredited, only that they collect recovery data. In the best of all worlds, the state would collect this data for all addiction treatment centers as they can be consistent and honest.

I am pretty sure I could pose as a family physician and get good ratings. I would be on schedule, listen carefully, and be on a first name basis with my patients. I would recommend a healthy diet, exercise, plenty of sleep, methods for stress relief and lots of placebos. I might even prescribe a few medicines recommended by the many pharmaceutical reps that drop by my office. For people with serious problems, I would refer them to specialists which would only convince my patients that I am a doctor without a big ego.

I had an aunt who was brilliant. Her college advisor told her she could be anything she wanted to be. She chose to be a social worker. She lived a modest life attending classes at the University of Minnesota throughout her life. I would like to see social workers compared to psychologists and physicians. I believe that social workers are more likely to choose a life of service than psychologists or physicians. Counseling psychologists do not even want a web site to improve their services, let alone pre and post testing. Physicians create schedules where they are late for appointments 80% of the time. Seinfeld once had a show where the doctor required payment if you did not cancel within 24 hours but you received nothing if the doctor cancelled (emergency?) for your appointment.

Epilogue

Clearly, some occupations let you rise to the top on merit more than others. At the same time several other factors are involved in a person's vocational success such as certificates and licenses, beauty, social skills and personality. Overall, it appears to me that people skills are often more relevant that job skills if you want to rise to the top.

No doubt a lot of chance events occur in all of our lives. For example, the death or retirement of a supervisor might produce an opening, an employee might leave for another job, or you are just in the right place at the right time. Of course chance and timing can actually work against you. I was offered a federal psychologist job in Santa Fe, New Mexico until someone in Albuquerque decided to transfer. When I eventually took a federal job as a GS-9 to automate tracking medical personnel, no one told me that I could no longer apply for GS-12 and GS-13 positions. Once you take a job in the federal government, you are only qualified for the next level position even if that position is in a completely different occupation.

Now that you have reached the end of my book I can admit that I did very little research for this book (as if you didn't already know). I wrote from personal experience and looked up a lot of facts on the internet. I am sure when I got to your occupation you had a lot of disagreement with me. As mentioned previously, I did two years of research for my first book that sold about two copies per month until I got a great review and my sales shriveled up. I wasn't going to make that mistake again. I figured this time I would go for entertainment and personal experiences and you would let a lot of my mistakes slide.

Whereas I hope I gave you something to think about when choosing an occupation, I must admit I had other reasons for writing this book. For one thing, it has never been clear to me why I was passed over for so many positions as a psychologist. Even with psychology being low on the merit scale, I feel that I had a rather impressive resume. I made it to the second interview for a position evaluating the state hospitals in Texas. Considering that I had initiated and chaired a two day conference on program evaluation for the state of Minnesota, I believe I was clearly the most experienced of their applicants. I can only guess that I was not chosen because they did not like me. To make matters worse, this was not even a clinical position. It required technical skills.

I am pretty sure that I interview poorly. Before leaving Brainerd State Hospital, I applied for the chief psychologist position at another Minnesota State hospital. When I went for an interview, the retiring chief psychologist recommended me for the job. So did the chief psychologist for the state of Minnesota. My competition was a man who wore a sport jacket over a turtle necked sweater, smoked a pipe, and spoke in a slow contemplative voice. I was doomed. I am normally a quiet introverted person but I get very animated in an interview. I want to answer questions that were never asked. I am like a musician who changes personalities when on the stage. Furthermore, I do not have good eye contact, a habit I have found difficult to break. When I left the interview room I heard someone say "He looks so young!"

In writing this book, it became clear to me that my problem was not in the skills I had. My problem was in an important skill I did not have – marketing. If I had to do it over again, I would have found someone who would help me do mock job interviews. I could have corrected my body language including eye contact. I would have responded to their questions without having so many questions of my own. I would have tailored my resume to each job application. Most of all, I would <u>not</u> have told the interviewers how I was going to improve upon their operation even though "What can you do for us?" is one of the five questions the book *What Color is Your Parachute* says you <u>must</u> answer.

I should have made friends with a psychologist who already had more than one book published. I could have received tips on how to present my book and possibly a contact in the publishing industry. It is difficult to get an agent if you have never published.

After retiring, instead of volunteering at a food bank, I should have volunteered at a local community theater. I was actually in the play "How to Succeed in Business without Really Trying" when I worked as a psychologist in Brainerd Minnesota. Perhaps I could have found a director who would have at least read one of my plays.

Obviously, I am not the only person who has learned you cannot make it through this life by being book smart. Perhaps, it was my lack of people skills that made psychology a poor occupational choice for me in the first place.

The good news is that when applying for a job in data processing, the poorer your interview goes, the smarter they think you are. Of course I am referring to the early 1980's when most people good with computers tended to be loners who were self-taught. I could have skipped college and went right into data processing by teaching myself FORTRAN (which I did anyway). I would have had a ten year head start over Bill Gates. I may not have been a Bill Gates but I could have made a good living automating businesses.

Another problem I had with psychology is that counseling and testing is not my forte. Planning and organization is where I excel. Unfortunately for me, these tend to be high level jobs that you get by working your way up the ladder. Had I stayed in Minnesota I might have replaced their chief psychologist who I knew well. I had plans for integrating mental health centers with state hospitals. I thought the state should have a means of tracking what becomes of people involved in their services long before database software was available.

In Texas I blame a part of my poor interviewing with my Minnesota background. For one thing, I was completely honest. I had no conception of trying to look good on an interview. Furthermore, I marketed myself, not as someone who is going to fit in, but as someone who is going to improve things. I applied for the position of Employee Assistance Coordinator with the city of San Antonio. I sent them a resume (see Appendix 15) tailored to described my experience for each of the job skills they wanted. Unfortunately, I included potential actions I would take in this position. Evidently, this arrogance offended them. To my surprise at the time, I was never invited for an interview. I did, however, receive a letter thanking me for my application. The letter explained that "Interviews are granted only to those best suited for the position."

Another reason for writing this book is I see it as my last chance to do something of value relating to my background in psychology. After spending two years writing "Counseling: A Profession or a Trade?" I did not expect such a minimal response, especially with so many people in counseling or knowing of someone in counseling. My hope is that this book will appeal to more people. Perhaps I can keep some of the people who read this book from making my same mistakes.

The final reason for me writing this book is that it gave me a chance to sneak in my autobiography, especially within the appendices. It allowed me to write from my life experiences instead of a summary of journal articles. Unfortunately, this no doubt made me appear at times to be way off track. I hope you appreciated at least some of my ramblings. Writing this book has allowed me to look back on what I have done in the field of psychology and elsewhere. I feel bad for all of those people with problems of addiction. I was hoping to make a lasting contribution in this field. Perhaps I did enough with my education to be worth the effort. Although this book is probably the termination of my work in psychology, I have not yet given up on my music. I will continue to compose music and hope for one of my musicals will be produced.

If we were put on this earth to learn a lesson, mine would have to be about status. How many people have went from a promising professional career to sweeping floors and washing dishes without having suffered a major loss or having an addiction or other serious medical problem? I treat everyone as deserving respect because I realize that I am in no position to judge others. I know that one major event or decision can change your life. Furthermore, in addition to alcoholism, some members of my family tree are manic depressive. Sometimes at night my mind races and I cannot sleep. I am probably one gene away from being an entirely different person. God sends rain on the just and the unjust. Fortunately God does the same with love.

Team spirit is based on recognizing the value of everyone on the team. Football teams need it and so do orchestras. We broke up the hierarchy at Brainerd State Hospital by having a counselor/patient based system. We had a great program for schizophrenics called "Tea Time" when they would meet as a group to help develop their social skills. This program was created and run by a psychiatric technician! One of the best things about Alcoholics Anonymous is a sponsor; someone you can count on when you are not in a good place. A former addict came up with an app for keeping people connected to their former place of treatment (Sparkite).

Good ideas for any business do not necessarily come from management. Businesses need profit sharing and loss sharing to show that everyone is valued. They need teams that are not run by the senior person. They need managers that come to you on occasion to chat. They need a system of rewards and recognition for good ideas and also for people or groups of people who go out of their way to help.

Hospitals and doctor's offices seem to go out of their way to be totalitarian organizations. Here are my suggestions to improve morale:

(1) Get rid of the "doctor" title.
(2) Medical staff should dress in normal clothes when possible.
(3) Create an app that tells how late the doctor is running. If I know my doctor is running 45 minutes late, I can come 30 minutes late for my appointment.
(4) Television and magazines are nice for the waiting room but how about free coffee and something to eat. I get that waiting for my car to be repaired.
(5) Do not let the nurse take you to a private room to take your vitals unless the doctor is ready to see you. Most people consider solitary confinement to be a punishment.
(6) There are plenty of unskilled people out of work. Hospitals can afford to pay someone minimum wage to push people around in wheelchairs. If you want to be a volunteer, go to a nursing home where money is tight. Also consider making people who cannot pay their bills do "volunteer" work.
(7) How about advertising your prices? What is the price of an office visit? What medical procedures do you do and what do they cost? I cannot find a single person who considered cost when choosing a primary physician.
(8) Join the elite group of physicians who do not accept any gifts from sales people including pharmaceutical reps.

Our criminal justice system is in the dark ages compared to medicine. Do you think voting for a hospital administrator would improve medical care? Do you think that a committee of various outsiders should determine who is ready to leave the hospital? I could write a computer program that would do better than any parole board and it would get better over time. All I have to do is determine what factors are related to recidivism.

No point in putting the best judges in charge of felonies. Let's elect a judge with a good-looking family who goes to church regularly and is tough on crime. Of course, the same goes for the sheriff. Couldn't we at least limit voting to people who work in law enforcement?

When it comes to Supreme Court justices, what counts most is the person's "philosophy". And we certainly do not want someone who legislates from the bench. I've got a computer program for that too. A computer can review the past to make sure we do what we have always done, even if it makes things worse. And God forbid we have a "Drug Czar" with an advanced degree in the social sciences. Let's give this job to someone who contributed to the last election.

I am serious when I say I would major in the theater if I wanted to be a politician or any other job that requires being elected. Merit is certainly a factor in politics. The best actors get elected.

Let me end on a more positive note. Everyone has merit in some way or another. Perhaps that is one reason for not emphasizing it in an occupation. On the other hand, most everyone wants to do what they are best at. I thought I was pretty knowledgeable about psychology. I leave you with this parting thought. Knowledge is great in a job but wouldn't you rather have nice friends than smart ones?

Appendix 1

Counselor Evaluation by the Client

J. Alexander Wieriman

(An Example: To be done anonymously on-line)

Name of your Counselor: _____

    Today's Date: M __ D __ Y __

Approximate number of weeks you were in counseling:

_____

Your Sex: M __ F __   Your Age Range: Below 20 __
20-29 __ 30-39 __ 40-59 __ Over 60 __

First Time in Counseling? Y __ N __

Answer the following questions according to this guide:

1 = Never, 2 = Seldom, 3 = Sometimes, 4 = Often, 5 = Always

    1. Did your counselor make you feel comfortable? __
    2. Was your counselor a good listener? __
    3. Was your counselor judgmental? __
    4. Did your counselor give advice? __
    5. Did your counselor assign homework? __
    6. Did your counselor help you set goals? __
    7. Did your counselor explain his or her approach to counseling? Y __ N __
    8. Did your counselor ask to speak with someone who knows you? Y __ N __
    9. Did your counselor work with you on developing exit criteria (i.e., what needs to happen that will make you ready for discharge?) Y __ N __

10. Did your counselor do any kind of testing?
    Y __ N __
11. Did your counselor chart or make you keep track of any specific behaviors? Y __ N __
12. Did your counselor refer you to any other source of assistance? Y __ N __

Answer the following questions according to this guide:

1 = not at all, 2 = very little, 3 = somewhat, 4 = very much, 5 = extremely

13. How knowledgeable would you rate your counselor? __
14. How helpful would you rate your counselor? __

Comments:

_____

_____

_____

_____

_____

If you are an entrepreneur, you might want to create a "Counselor Evaluation by the Client" for your state. You can get a list of licensed counselors from your state licensing board. Given that evaluations such as these are already being done for physicians, I expect the only legal ramifications are to be a licensed internet business. I have consulted physician ratings myself. I typically need a minimum of five ratings (preferably ten) before I pay any attention to them.

As I have said before, I know very little about marketing. You will have to figure out how to get clients of counselors to fill out your counselor evaluations. There are probably several people who can help you with this task. Furthermore, there might be a bias in who fills out these evaluations. Perhaps the disgruntled are more likely to respond. My biggest concern is that counselors will encourage their clients to give them favorable ratings.

For what it is worth, you could publish some of your results in respectable journals. For example, how is giving advice related to how helpful the counselor is rated? It would be my guess that "never" giving advice or "always" giving advice would receive lower ratings on item 14 (helpfulness). Periodically, you could add a special question just for research purposes. Examples of research questions include:

(1) Were you pressured to go into counseling? (Yes, No)
(2) Was your counseling better or worse than expected? (Better, Worse, Neither)
(3) How did you choose your counselor? (Recommended by a friend, Recommended by your physician, Chosen via the internet, Picked at random, Other)
(4) Did your counselor make any inappropriate remarks or gestures? (Yes, No)
(5) Did your counseling last: Shorter than expected? Longer than expected? Neither?)

Most studies on counseling have sample sizes from 20 to 40 people. With internet ratings you might have a sample size of several hundred people.

So how will you make money? I suggest you first try to sell ad space to pharmaceutical companies that sell antidepressants and anti-anxiety medications. These companies have megabucks!

Are you a people person? Are you older? Possibly retired or tired of your present job? Consider becoming a life coach. There are courses plus mentoring to make you a certified life coach. However, there are presently no state requirements. First of all, if you think I am looking for someone with a lot of life experiences to give advice, please go on to the next appendix. Let me give you my personal experience with advice.

When I was much younger, I went to a licensed Ph.D. counselor because I had trouble meeting women. He suggested I place an ad in a local paper under men seeking woman. He also advised that I should include everything I was looking for in a woman. Guess what? I did not receive a single reply! The readers probably thought that I was too fussy. He never even apologized to me for giving bad advice.

The reason counselors and life coaches should not give advice is because it shifts the responsibility from the client to the counselor. Had we discussed possible things I could do to meet a woman, we might have included a personal ad. We would have the discussed the possible consequences, good and bad. Then the decision would be up to me. If the consequences were unfavorable, we would discuss this and hopefully I would learn something. Even if your advice is great, you just convinced your client that he is helpless or stupid and needs to go to someone smarter when a decision needs to be made. Is this your idea of counseling? Good counselors are facilitators, not advice givers.

I am looking for an older person because I am looking for someone who had a lot of failures but learned from them and persevered. Thomas Edison was called the "Wizard of Menlo Park". He should have been called the "Failure of Menlo Park". He was working at the age of 16, never having finished high school. His teachers said he was too stupid to learn anything. He was fired from his first two jobs. Thomas Edison created over 1000 failed light bulbs. If you had a history of failures before you got it right, you are my candidate for life coach. The world is full of counselors who were never broke, never divorced, never addicted, and were never fired from a job

It is just a matter of time before the state licenses life coaches. Of course you will have to take the official classes and possibly pass a test. On the good side, you might be grandfathered in if you have been a life coach for "x" amount of time.

I deliberately placed my conversation about a life coach after my "Counselor Evaluation by the Client". If you become a life coach, you will begin by documenting the person's problem areas and/or goals set. You will then have the client do an evaluation at the end of your services and six months later. Before the state will license life coaches, they will have hearings, some open to the public. You will go before them with a summary of your evaluations. You will then say "Here is my evidence that I am able to help people as a life coach. Do you have any evidence that licensed counselors with Master degrees and Ph.D.'s do any better? Do you have any evidence that persons who took life coach training through the

International Coach Federation (ICF) do any better?" Of course the answer will be "no". You then suggest they collect evidence before making new regulations.

Appendix 2

Choosing a Counselor

J. Alexander Wieriman

Why the advice you have been given all of these years is wrong.

The New York Times recently had an article that noted many psychiatrists no longer act as counselors. Instead they primarily dispense prescriptions and make prescription adjustments. This leaves professional counseling primarily to psychologists and social workers. Furthermore, the article says that "There is no evidence that psychiatrists provide higher quality talk therapy than psychologists or social workers."

What the article does not tell you is that numerous studies over the past 40 years have shown that counselors with advanced degrees do not make better counselors than paraprofessionals, persons with less than a master's degree. In fact, quite a bit of evidence tends to favor the paraprofessionals. I will make only a brief mention of the many studies comparing professional counselors with paraprofessionals. The real question becomes why do so few people know that choosing a paraprofessional counselor, if you can find one, is a good choice.

As early as 1965 eight homemakers trained to conduct therapy were found to be as effective as trained professionals. By 1968, nearly 30 more comparison studies were done. One of the major researchers in this area concluded that lay trainees function at levels as high as or higher than professionals. The paraprofessionals also engage clients in the counseling process at levels as high as or higher than professional trainees.   In a review of 42 studies in 1979, one study favored the professionals, whereas twelve studies favored the paraprofessionals. A summarization of the literature in 1984 of studies that compared professionals with other counselors found 154 comparisons from 39 studies. These studies indicate that the clients who seek help from paraprofessionals are more likely to achieve resolution of their problems than those who consult professionals. Furthermore, they noted the highest quality studies favored the paraprofessionals. I am not familiar with any current research that alters these conclusions.

Clearly we cannot expect academia to have an interest in paraprofessional counselors. Academia is in the business of turning out counseling graduates with advanced degrees. According to the Bureau of Labor Statistics, there were 113,300 mental health counselors in 2008. The fifty states have already decided, without convincing evidence, on a process for licensing counselors. According to Wikipedia, all 50 states acknowledge a Licensed Professional Counselor (LPC). To become an LPC you need at least a master's degree, you must pass the National Counselors Exam, and do an internship that requires working many hours under supervision. Surprisingly, even Wikipedia states that no controlled study has ever found a difference in effectiveness between therapists of different education levels or licensure.

According to the National Board for Certified Counselors (www.nbcc.org), the purpose of the National Counselor Examination (NCE, also the Examination for the Professional Practice of Psychology - the EPPP) is to assess knowledge, skills, and abilities viewed as important for providing effective counseling services. The NCE is comprised of 200 multiple choice questions. I play the trumpet in a community band. If I could have my music skills assessed by a multiple choice test, I could be playing in a major symphony orchestra. Unfortunately, they would probably actually want to hear me play the trumpet first. Couldn't we at least videotape prospective counselors doing actual counseling and have them assessed by independent raters as a part of the licensing requirements? Of course, if the independent raters cannot agree with each other, i.e. show a high correlation, we have a more serious problem.

The major problem with counseling, as I see it, is that counseling is not primarily an evidence-based occupation. Once you get your advanced degree and license, you can make a comfortable living whether you are able to help anyone or not. A Johns Hopkins review of 475 studies found that even years of experience had no relationship with therapy outcome. At one point in my life I applied for several jobs as a psychologist. I was never asked to provide evidence that I had changed a person's life for the better. The good news for counselors is that since most individuals seek counseling at the lowest points in their lives, they can only get better. Even if they do not improve by any objective measures, most clients will tell you they are better after counseling.

Besides working as a psychologist, I have also worked as a computer programmer, which is a very evidence-based occupation. I was able to automate the tracking of 16,000 military medical personnel, which resulted in a savings of 500 man-hours per month. I did this without a single computer science class to my name. Bill Gates and Mark Zuckerberg have already demonstrated that it is possible to do well in this field without a college degree.

Based upon the research literature and other considerations (see my book *"Counseling: A Profession or a Trade?"* an Amazon e-book), I recommend we first identify people who would make good counselors (i.e., good listeners, empathetic, nonjudgmental with a wide range of experiences) and then train them. This training would be a type of trade school, as I do not expect the "naturals" to necessarily be blessed with the ability to pass a statistics course and do research. A small number of schools do offer counseling certificates to those with less than a master's degree but these jobs seldom, if ever, involve traditional 50 minute counseling sessions.

Of course we would still need the professionals to set up counseling programs, train and monitor counselors, and do psychological testing and program evaluation. And yes, some of these same people might even make good counselors.

Writing a book on counseling does not make that person a good counselor any more than writing a great screen play makes that person a good actor. Good counseling requires more than knowledge.

(Further Reading)

Differential Functioning of Lay and Professional Helpers. Carkuff and Truax in *Journal of Consulting Psychology,* 1968, vol.15.

Comparative Effectiveness of Paraprofessional and Professional Helpers. Durlak in *Psychological Bulletin*, 1979, vol. 86.

Comparative Effectiveness of Professional and Paraprofessional Helpers. Hattie in *Psychological Bulletin*, 1984, vol. 95.

Appendix 3

Counseling – It's not Rocket Science

TED TALK Proposal

J. Alexander Wieriman

My name is Jay. I am here to talk about counseling. Counseling is big business. In the United States there are over 120,000 licensed counselors treating millions of Americans. I do not have a lot of respect for counselors. They have a lot of fuzzy skills with little proof they are effective. On the other hand, I like automotive mechanics. They get certificates in specific systems like brakes, transmissions, air conditioning and they guarantee your car will run better.

Counseling is like no other job. For example, the poorer you do your job the more money you make. Think about it. If your clients never get better, they stay with you until they get exasperated or their money runs out.

Inept physicians can lose their licenses. There are a lot of serious ways a physician can screw up from prescribing the wrong medicine to cutting off the wrong leg. A counselor has to abuse or seduce a patient to lose his or her license. To my knowledge no counselor has ever lost a certified counselor's license for being incompetent. That's even better than a federal job.

This brings us to another benefit of being a counselor. If your client doesn't get better you can blame the client. How sweet is that? Have you ever had an auto mechanic tell you "If you had a Ford it would be fixed already but those Chevys are known to be uncooperative"?

Most counselors have no idea of their success rate. I worked with alcoholics in my younger day. I enjoy asking counselors in addiction treatment programs what their success rate is. I had one young fellow tell me it was 80% for those who stick with the program. I gave a speech once to a VA hospital and told them that I had a 100% success rate for those who stuck with my alcohol addiction program. I could see they thought I was kidding so I said "this is really true." Now that I had their attention I continued. "Here is my program. I sit across the desk from a patient, look him in the eye and I say 'don't drink.'" Everyone who follows my program gets better.

When do people seek out a counselor? People might seek counseling when depressed, anxious, or having relationship problems. However, usually a person does not seek out a counselor until he or she has reached an all-time low. This is good news for counselors because most of your clients are going to get better no matter what you do. What a great job! Have you ever heard a garage mechanic say "I think I will leave your car in the back for a few days. Let's see if it will get better on its own."

Another perk of being a counselor is that clients will say they are getting better even when they are not. This can be explained by a combination of cognitive dissonance, expectations and the placebo effect. The theory of cognitive dissonance says that no one wants to pay for months of counseling and then admit it was worthless. That would make them not only crazy but stupid. That's a combination I would like to avoid.

If I had ten depressed clients, I could tell them they were short of dopamine. I could then say that standing on your head for an hour a day increases your level of dopamine. Three months later most of my clients would tell me they were feeling better. That is the power of a placebo. Some counselors are masters at manipulating a person's expectations. If you have studied anthropology, we call these people shamans. For the rest of you, we call them charlatans.

Academic psychologists who study counseling use control groups to cancel out the placebo effect. Unfortunately, waiting for therapy is not a very good control group. What I would like to see are clients randomly assigned to either a certified counselor or to a person with a degree in English, Accounting, Engineering, etc. with a plaque on the wall that says he or she is a certified counselor. I wonder how the clients would differ after six months. On the other hand I have a pretty good idea of what would happen if I gave an English major a box of tools and told him to fix my car.

Another perk of counseling is that you get to work in a cozy air-conditioned office. A counselor with an advanced degree might give you a number you can text or call in case of an emergency but she's probably not coming over to your home in the middle of the night. Doctors no longer make house calls.

I worked in a psychiatric hospital. Hospitals have the same problems as conventional counseling. In both cases you are dealing with people in a highly controlled environment. Hospitals are safe places but will any gains made there hold up when the patient returns home? We had two VISTA volunteers who met with our patients after discharge to see if they were following up on their goals created while in treatment. "Time Structuring" received an award from the National Institute of Drug Abuse.

Most addiction programs tell patients to avoid situations that could lead to drinking. One of our activities had a counselor and VISTA volunteer take a few of our patients to a bar at night. You heard me. They went to a bar where they would order soft drinks, play pool, and dance. For those of you who studied psychology, we were using the tried and true principles of desensitization and exposure and response prevention. I still believe this is an effective way to deal with a drinking problem. Any day now, this practice is going to catch on. Of course I am kidding. It will never catch on. It involves working at night, leaving the treatment center, and worrying about what insurance covers if something goes wrong. Best we treat people in an artificial setting.

So maybe a client has problems with his wife, his kids, the neighbors or most of his co-workers. No need to run to his home or office. You will simply take your client's word for everything. Does that make sense? The person is disturbed enough to want counseling but you assume his or her story is an accurate representation of reality. Someone told me once that it isn't important if the story is true; only if the client believes it. My response was "If you don't have independent verification that your client is honest, how do you know if he really believes it?" This isn't as far-fetched as it sounds. Some people are coerced into counseling by a spouse or employer. These people might think that lying is in their best interest.

I believe counseling needs what is called consensual validation. Is a client delusional or are people really out to get him? We need the opinions of others. At the very least a counselor should invite others who know the client to come down to her air-conditioned office.

One interesting fact about counseling is that counselors do not get better with experience. A Johns Hopkins review of 475 studies found that years of experience had no relationship with therapy outcome. In other words, if you are fresh out of college, you are as good as you are going to get. Fortunately, this finding is easy to explain. There is only one way to get better at anything. It's called feedback. How could you improve at shooting a gun if you had no idea where your bullets were going? You need a measurable target. When an auto mechanic hears the sound of an engine running smoothly he knows the carburetor is fixed.

Both counselors and their clients need valid feedback. If you are looking for someone who can really change a person's behavior, try a salesperson. If you are in sales, you learn what works or you starve. Politicians and motivational speakers are also good at changing behaviors by manipulating our emotions. Their jobs depend on this. Bill Clinton is an expert. Counselors don't have to improve and I expect many don't.

At the psychiatric hospital in Minnesota where I worked, we sent out a form to be filled out by a significant other for every patient who came through our doors. We sent out the form upon the patient's admission to our hospital and one month and again at six months after his or her release. This provided us feedback on the success of our programs. We also monitored our readmission rates. When a patient left the hospital, he or she filled out a form indicating the activities the patient found most helpful. Although medications and counseling were the big winners, every activity on our form received a number one spot from at least one person. Tell that to someone who doesn't think recreation is real therapy. Furthermore, patients who left against medical advice did as well as everyone else. There is no way to know that without follow-up. In part because of our evaluation efforts, our hospital became one of only seven multiservice hospitals in the United States be become fully accredited at that time.

What if licensure for counseling required every client to have a standard follow-up form by a significant other like we used at our hospital? With the internet, this form would go to a centralized database as well as the counselor. With a little data mining the potential for improving counseling would be enormous.

Even better, what if states provided for independent centers to diagnose and refer people for counseling. These same centers could do pre and post follow-up to determine who the good counselors are. Unlike the mental health centers of today, it would be important that these referral centers maintain their integrity by not doing any counseling.

I attended the University of Minnesota. Had I followed my dream, as TED speakers are fond of telling you, I would have been either writing movies scores or living above a garage. Instead I studied psychology. In my day the University of Minnesota was called the center of dustbowl empiricism. I am a behaviorist. I believe in charting behaviors. Common behaviors a counselor might deal with include AA attendance, hours of sleep, husband and wife alone time, time spent with the children, number of cigarettes smoked, time exercising, hours of television watched, time spent on a hobby. The behaviorist motto is "If you can measure it, you can change it."

In the "Time Structuring" program, we limited the number of conversations about drinking or drug use. We relied on role playing to see how our patients responded to various real life situations. It was my impression that a lot of patients were good talkers but did not do nearly so well when handling that same situation role playing. Sometimes we would have a patient switch roles. He might play his spouse or his counselor. It was always interesting to see what a patient in the role of a counselor would tell himself.

I am a big believer in skills. I taught a relaxation class including what today would be called mindfulness. I taught visualization for achieving goals. I also taught active listening, a skill used by counselors. One of the strangest skills I taught was walking. Yes, I said walking. Have you ever seen a depressed person walk? I taught depressed patients to walk with their heads high and their arms swinging at their sides. There is good evidence that our mood not only affects our body language but that our body language affects our mood. Everybody up. Now jump around and act silly. There, don't you feel better. You may sit down. Hitler was right. You can get a crowd to do just about anything.

Although I am primarily a behaviorist, there are plenty of studies that support a variety of therapies. I had a conversation once with Albert Ellis. He developed one of the first cognitive therapies called Rational Emotive Therapy. He introduced the concepts of "musturbation" and catastrophizing.

"I must get all A's. I must get into medical school. I must become a doctor. Otherwise, I will be a complete failure."

Interviewing for a psychologist's position is quite interesting. I have applied for many jobs as a psychologist and was never, I repeat, never asked for evidence that I could change someone's behavior. Instead I was asked "What tests do you administer?" At the psychiatric hospital where I worked, we gave everyone the MMPI – the Minnesota Multiphasic Personality Inventory. Sure this test is better than the magic ink spots but does it help anyone get better?

In my opinion, one of the least helpful things a psychiatric facility can do is to give someone a fancy diagnosis. I believe we need more in-depth discussions with the referring party as to what unusual behaviors the person is exhibiting. Psychiatric facilities need a ticket of admission. Depression gets you in. Being unhappy doesn't. Hearing voices gets you in. Being unemployed doesn't. That is why a family won't tell you they are tired of living with this slob who won't get a job. Sure, he may be schizophrenic but unfortunately, reducing his schizophrenia won't necessarily lead to a clean room and a job.

I think the main purpose of psychological testing is to have a nice page in the patient's medical record. I believe in interviews and observations. Let me say I am all for psychological tests that help you make treatment decisions. I would have loved to have had a paper and pencil test that indicated whether a particular schizophrenic would benefit from medication. This would have saved us a tremendous amount of time and effort.

Of course I am all for behavior checklists. Most tests for depression are actually behavior checklists. They ask questions like

Do you have trouble sleeping?

Has your appetite changed?

Has your sex life diminished?

Do you spend less time on a hobby?

So how do you get to be a licensed counselor?

First, you need to get a master's degree or higher. Second, you need 3000 hours of supervision. Third, you need to pass the National Counselor Examination which consists of 200 multiple choice questions; no video tapes of actual counseling, just multiple choice questions. Holy Cow, with a degree in music and a multiple choice test, I could be playing for a major symphony orchestra.

So who makes the best counselors? Psychiatrists? Psychologists? Social workers? Raise your hand if you know the answer? This question was answered in the 1980's. It's just that nobody cares. Paraprofessionals make the best counselors, that is, people with less than a master's degree. Let me repeat that. The best counselors are people with less than a master's degree. And yes, you cannot be a certified counselor with less than a master's degree. Does anyone see a problem here? For anyone who wants to verify this fact, it is not on the Internet. You need to go to your local university where you can read the journal articles. You might want to start with the Psychological Bulletin, 1984, volume 95. At the hospital where I worked, we had three counselors for chemical dependency and three counselors for the mentally ill. Four of those counselors had bachelor degrees and two of the counselors were recovering alcoholics with no college degrees.

If you do not mind a little bragging, I wrote a book on counseling. I have a Ph.D. with 96 semester credit hours in psychology. I took the test in psychology as part of the Graduate Record Exam and scored two levels above the 99th percentile. Guess what? I am not a good counselor. I am a talker, not a listener. (Note: I am only a talker when it comes to the social sciences.) For our "Time Structuring" program I hired a man with a degree in recreation to be our counselor. He was friendly, a good listener, empathetic, and nonjudgmental. Even better, he knew all about hunting and fishing in northern Minnesota.

Knowing the theory of counseling and applying it are two different things. Thinking you are a good counselor because you wrote a textbook on counseling is like thinking because you wrote a screen play, you could play the lead.

How many of you have had surgery? A good surgeon requires excellent hand to eye coordination, physical stamina for long operations, and unflappable emotions to handle emergency situations. Guess what? None of those abilities are measured on the MCAT, the test to get into medical school. Is that scary or what? Counseling is just one of many occupations that requires more than book learning.

Is it possible to have a Ph.D. in psychology and be a good counselor? Is it possible for an 'A' student to be a good football player? Harvard won the Rose Bowl in 1920. Guess how many bowl games they have been in since. (Make a zero with your hand.)

I have the following theory – If you are not a good counselor by the time you are eighteen you will never be a great counselor. For example, talkers should not be counselors. Do you think you can get a natural talker to be a listener for eight hours a day? I don't. Can you teach a person to be compassionate and empathetic? I have yet to see a psychology class titled Empathy 1. Can you train people to be nonjudgmental? Boy that would be great. I would give out gift certificates for Christmas.

In summary, I believe that counseling should be a trade and not a profession. We should take people with "natural" counseling ability right out of high school and teach them counseling skills from cognitive therapy, behavioral therapy, interpersonal therapy, family therapy, the addictions, and so forth. Give them certificates for each specialty mastered much like auto mechanics get certificates. Of course they would have to call themselves "life coaches" to avoid problems with the state.

Do we need PhD's for counseling? Do we need engineers to work on cars? Look, it's counseling; it's not rocket science. Thank you.

Appendix 4

Measuring Racial Prejudice over Time with Home Buying

Serious incidences of shootings and burnings vary considerably in their frequency over time to be a meaningful long term measure of racial prejudice. Looking at minority presidents or member of Congress would only suggest that Native Americans and Inuits (Eskimos) are the most discriminated people in the United States. Furthermore, we are one of the few countries that was never governed by a woman, especially when women make up a majority of voters. Measures of police arrests and sentencing reflect primarily the lower classes. Studies of discrimination against potential renters or job applicants usually only show one sided discrimination. Plus this type of discrimination probably reflects skin color more than race.

The National Institute of Health summarizes 16 measure of racism (https://www.ncbi.nlm.nih.gov/pmc/articles/PMC4389587/). These measures represent subjectively perceived racism. The majority of these measures meet the various statistical considerations of validity and reliability.

A more direct measure of prejudice involves measuring response time. For example, does a white person see a gun held by a black person more quickly than a gun held by a white person? Does this response time differ from that of a black person? The "Implicit Association Test" is one such measure although supporting evidence is weak for this test. The problem with measures like these is they appear to measure the prejudice of white people better than the prejudice of black people or Asians or Hispanics. Furthermore, the fact that white people are not afraid of Asians with guns does not mean they are not prejudice against Asians in other ways.

Another way to gauge racial prejudice is to look at the percent of interracial marriages in recent years, such as the last 30 years. However, a black educated woman might prefer a black man but finds a white suitor to be more readily available.

Clearly, any measure of segregation across time needs to look at <u>voluntary</u> segregation. Consequently, forcing minorities to travel across town to go to school is of no value. Looking at churches might be one way to look at voluntary segregation. However, children usually like the kind of church service similar to where they went as a child. Going to a church where the sermon is in Spanish does not quality as prejudice. Neither does going to a church where the congregation is very vocal or the music very lively. New Orleans is proud of our black Catholic University. Are black Catholics really that different than white Catholics? This looks like a case of separate but equal to me.

Segregation in housing seems to be one of the best measure of determining if the United States is becoming less racially prejudice over time, especially when people have a choice of where to live. I remember being in Houston Texas in the 1970's and being told that Houston was proud to be one of the first cities to have a rich black neighborhood. Why would anyone be proud that people who could live anywhere would chose to segregate?

195

The Census Bureau is the source for most studies on housing segregation. They list 10 measures (https://www.census.gov/hhes/www/housing/resseg/pdf/app_b.pdf). Unfortunately, none of these measures of housing segregation takes into account socio-economic status. No matter what race you belong to, poor people cannot move into rich neighborhoods. Hopefully, someone will modify these models for that purpose.

Logan and Parman wrote a recent paper on "Measuring Residential Segregation" (March 24, 2014) that includes rural areas and therefore covers the entire United States. They say that their measure of segregation is not as influenced by boundaries as previous measures. As economists and not psychologists, their measure is geared toward correlating segregation of blacks with health and economic data. In other words, there interest is not primarily in measuring prejudice.

Most studies on housing segregation rely on Census Data because statisticians love large samples. Suppose someone in Boston includes New Orleans in his study. Suppose the data shows that segregation in housing is a lot less now than it was over ten years ago. Do they know that hurricane Katrina obliterated a poor black neighborhood? Do they know that many blacks needed to move into mostly white Metairie to find housing? Do they know that some whites fled to the Northshore to live in an all-white neighborhood? In other words, it is quite possible that white/black prejudice in New Orleans has not improved in spite of what the census housing data shows. Consequently, I believe census data alone is inadequate without some knowledge of the growth patterns of a particular city.

I worked on a research project on tri-ethnic segregation in housing in Austin, Texas in the 1970's. At that time the literature indicated that the United States in general was not making any gains in desegregation. Instead, as the population of cities were growing, large transition areas gave the <u>appearance</u> of desegregation. In a circular city this area of transition is larger than for a city built along a river. Furthermore, if gentrification occurs around the city center, the poor people in the second concentric ring have two transition areas to make desegregation appear even stronger. Can you see the irony in this? Kicking poor black people out of their inner city homes makes it appear that the city is less segregated.

There are ways for a study to try to correct for factors that affect housing segregation that are not related to prejudice. For example, you could compare a smaller city to a larger city whose housing patterns looked like this smaller city ten years ago. We would hope that the new small city would be less segregated.

I believe the best way to measure prejudice is to look at persons who moved into a single dwelling city house during the year. These people had a choice of picking a neighborhood. Of course some whites will say they wanted a low crime area and some blacks will say they did not want to live in a neighborhood where they were not wanted. Unless they can provide data from this new city to back up these ideas, these ideas represent prejudice.

Clearly we have to adjust for income. We can estimate this by looking at the taxes on the homes they purchased. If 70% of the people with a comparably priced home are white, then a random selection of a home in this price range would have 70% white neighbors.

It would be nice if we knew why a person moved into a new neighborhood. If their company transferred them from another city, their choice of neighborhood could easily reflect prejudice. If they moved to be close to relatives, they may not be prejudiced. Picking a house near a mall, park, hospital or good school are reasons for any race. By looking at a large number of homes purchased in a calendar year, I expect racial prejudices will show through.

The bottom line is that I believe we can measure racial prejudice for most cities by looking at buyers of homes during a calendar year and comparing the racial composition of their neighbors against base rates. The following example shows the data needed to compute this "Home Buyer Prejudice Index".

EXAMPLE for City "C"

Race of Home Buyer*: White, Black, Hispanic, Asian, Other/Mixed

Valuation of a home from taxes or another source. Given the value (V), one can compute a price range such as

Lower Price Range (LPR) = .9*V

Upper Price Range (UPR) = 1.1*V

If V = $200,000, LPR = $180,000; UPR = $220,000

Compute the racial distribution for people in city "C" with homes valued between $180,000 and $220,000:

Suppose: W = 72%, B = 12%, H= 8%, A = 3%, O = 5%.

N = the number of a home buyer's closest neighbors. Given this needs to be determined by a computer program, if his address is 3605 Jones St., you might consider everyone who lives between 3505 Jones St. and 3705 Jones St. to be his neighbors. GPS coordinates could also be used if available. If there is no simple way for a computer to determine at least 10 close neighbors, this homebuyer is excluded from the study.

If the homebuyer is white, compute the percent of neighbors who are white.

If this percent is over 72%, this person gets a +1.

If this percent is under 72%, this person gets a -1.

If the percent is about 72%, this person gets a 0.

Follow a similar procedure for the other races.

The above formulas have to be modified to include more zeros if the number of comparisons (N) is small. For example, with only 10 neighbors, the percent white can be 70% or 80% but not 72%. It would therefore make sense to give 70 % a zero instead of a minus one. Some races, such as Asians, may need to be excluded if their percent in a city is too small given the number of closest neighbors (N).

After computing a score for every new homebuyer with a sufficient number of neighbors, you average the scores to create a "Homebuyers Prejudice Index" for each race. Index scores can range from -1 to +1. The higher the score is above zero, the more prejudice in choosing a neighborhood. In the unlikely event the index is below zero, homebuyers are choosing to be in a diverse neighborhood.

Although statisticians have ways of comparing proportions, this should not be necessary after gathering 10 years or more of data. One should be able to look at a graph of ten years of the Home Buyer Prejudice Index to see if the index is rising, falling or remaining the same. Not only can you compare the prejudices among races within a city, you can compare the prejudices among cities with this proposed method. (Note: This index is still affected by transition areas.)

* The United States Census Department says "We ask about the characteristics of people who rent and people who own homes, such as age, gender, race, Hispanic origin, and disability status to help the government and communities enforce laws designed to eliminate discrimination in housing, such as the 1968 Fair Housing Act." They also ask for home value and the year moved in. However, "Individual records are not shared with anyone." https://www.census.gov/acs/www/about/why-we-ask-each-question/ownership/

Appendix 5

Levels of Dreaming

(Synopsis)

I use the following categories to classify dreams:

(1) Compiling

    (A) Residual

        Sleep allows you to discard a wealth of material that you processed during the day that is deemed of little value. A handful of people have what is called hyperthymesia. They can recall/relive what happened to them in the past. Most of these people consider this trait to be a burden. Residual dreams contain left over pieces from the day in a disjointed manner that are usually not interpretable.

    (B) Anxiety

        We all have unpleasant dreams of being chased, encountering sinister bodies, falling, hiding, violence or being punished. In the extreme, we call these dreams "nightmares". These dreams can speed up your heart and respiration so that you do not wake up feeling refreshed. This is your mind's way of dealing with stress in your life. (Today we refer to Post Traumatic Stress Syndrome). Anxiety dreams are not interpretable in the usual sense. You need to find out what is causing stress in your life and deal with it with your waking mind.

(2) Processing
  (A) Problem Solving
    If you have spent considerable time on a
    problem during the day, your dreams might
    continue this thought process. Many scientific
    discoveries came out of dreams such as the
    periodic table, the chemical structure of
    benzene and the transmission of nerves. Useful
    ideas that pop into your head may have come
    from a forgotten dream.
  (B) Wish Fulfillment
    Just as our fears are displayed in anxiety
    dreams, our hopes and desires are played out
    in our wish fulfillment dreams. You might
    dream of finding money, conversing with
    friends, or being in some exotic place. Sexual
    dreams are common. So are dreams with food.
    Seeing deceased relatives are usually at this
    level. Wish fulfillment dreams are often
    associated with Sigmund Freud. Freud believed
    that dreams were the royal road to the
    unconscious. He believed that dreams
    reflected repressed or unconscious desires.
  (C) Prophetic/Possibility
    Your mind evidently can analyze your
    circumstances and make future predictions.
    When I was hoping to go to the University of
    Oregon for my graduate work I had a dream
    than spelled out Texas. My most unusual
    dream was when I was given the word "Senf". I
    had never heard of the word but several years
    later I met a Janet Senf. Surprisingly, nothing
    came of that relationship. Some people believe

that deja vue experiences occur because you forgot that you previously had a dream about your present experience.

(3) Analyzing

   (A) Personal Symbolic

Dream books present various symbols and tell you what they mean. Whereas there is some truth is this, many dream symbols can only be interpreted by what they mean to the dreamer. For example, a dream about your uncle George might indicate that you are becoming arrogant like George. A dream about a house with faulty plumbing might signal a health problem relating to your body's plumbing or it might indicate an overflow of your emotions. Driving a car with no brakes might signal you are becoming out of control.

   (B) Universal Symbolic

Carl Jung believed in symbols common to most humans. He called these symbols archetypes. I had dreams of catching fish. This can be an archetype indicating spiritual food. Of course growing up in Minnesota, this could be a personal symbol. Assume symbols common to the human race such as water (emotions), circles (unity), and wild animals (danger) could be universal symbols in your dreams.

(4) Transcending

   (A) Soaring

Some dreams make you feel ecstatic. If you were awake you would be "in the zone" or flowing. For most people, these are dreams of flying and I do not mean in an airplane. I have dreams of skiing that are exhilarating and effortless. Some dreams have radiant colors. I had a dream of playing beautiful music on the piano that I had never heard before. Plus I do not play piano well when awake.

(B) Cosmic

Cosmic dreams usually have the mystical oneness feeling of being connected. In these dreams you just know that everything is right. I once had a dream of traveling through space and <u>seeing</u> the laws of the universe and noting which ones were stable and which ones were changing.

I recently had a dream where information was stored along a piece of wood. Not only would you need a key to decipher it, you would need to know it was not just an ordinary piece of wood. If this sounds far-fetched, read an article on quantum computing or on the DNA modifying technique called CRISPR.

Some people have lucid dreams when they are aware of dreaming which can give you a great sense of power. If you believe in astral travel you might visit places you have never been to before.

What makes my Levels of Dreaming unique is that it is not based on interpreting dreams. It is based on using it as a gauge as to how well you are doing. You may have thought that you had a good day but find yourself with anxiety dreams. You might have had a hectic day and have a soaring dream. The concept of Levels of Dreaming's best use is not to rely on a single night's dream but to look at your dreams over time. Improve your waking life and your dreaming life will reward you.

Your body has priority mechanisms to keep you healthy. For example, under conditions of starvation, your brain is the last organ to be deprived of nourishment. I believe that during sleep your mind begins with housekeeping tasks and then moves on to unfinished business that could include problem solving. When you reach the point of smooth sailing, your mind is free to play and perhaps soar.

Appendix 6

Regression to the Mean

Stock Market Strategy

Jay's Strategy for "Simple Percent Criteria" Day Trading   © Jalex, 2012

Change the parameters in bold and see what happens.   *Dates use the format '24-Jun-2009*

	First Date	Last Date
	3-Jan-2006	29-Jun-2012

Start

Strategy: If the S&P goes up **5.00%** I sell **10.00%** of my stock.
If the S&P goes down **4.00%** I buy **10.00%** new stock.

I will start on **03-Jan-2006** and end on **29-Jun-2012**

I start with **$10,000** in stocks and **$15,000** in cash.
Initial Assets $25,000

Results

Start Index	1,268.80				
End Index	1,362.16				
Index Gain	7.4%				

I will end with $30,780 in stocks
and $2,511 in cash.
Final Assets $33,291
Gain $8,291
For a period of 6.49 years.
Gain per year $1,277   5.1%

	# of Sells	9	Sells per yr	1.39
	# of Buys	21	Buys per yr	3.24
	Trades	30	Trds per yr	4.62
	No Cash for Buys	4		

Ave. Stock Value $18,999
Ave. Cash Value $8,113

Strategy Gain 33.2%
Difference 25.8%

If a trade costs	**$7.00** , cost of trades =	$210	Assets - Cost =	$33,162
If cash earns	**1.00%** , interest on cash =	$81	New Gain	32.6%
	Total Cost =	$129	Difference	25.3%

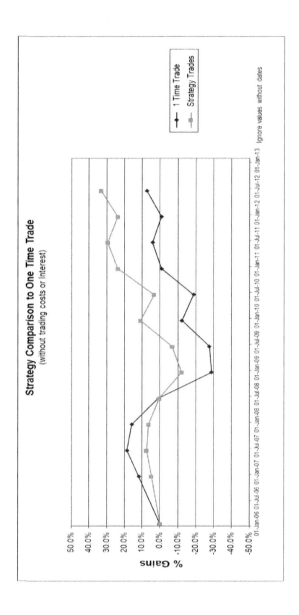

Strategy Comparison to One Time Trade
(without trading costs or Interest)

- 1 Time Trade
- Strategy Trades

Ignore values without dates

% Gains

50.0%
40.0%
30.0%
20.0%
10.0%
0.0%
-10.0%
-20.0%
-30.0%
-40.0%
-50.0%

01-Jan-06 01-Jul-06 01-Jan-07 01-Jul-07 01-Jan-08 01-Jul-08 01-Jan-09 01-Jul-09 01-Jan-10 01-Jul-10 01-Jan-11 01-Jul-11 01-Jan-12 01-Jul-12 01-Jan-13

Appendix 7

Selecting Leaders

J. Alexander Wieriman, Deputy Chief WCSC

This paper follows a presentation made to the New Orleans District on March 28, 2001 by psychologist Dr. Larry Hadfield of the Gallup Corporation.

First, I would like to commend the Corps for allocating the time and resources for an endeavor as worthwhile as selecting top leaders. Having worked for the Corps of Engineers for over fifteen years and having a background in psychology (Ph.D. from the University of Texas), I believe I am in a unique position to comment on the present selection process used by Gallup and the Corps.

First of all, the method used by Gallup of discovering items that correlate to a criterion is a tried and true process of creating psychological measurements. If anything, the profession of psychology has been criticized for having so many graduate students create measuring devices. What I intend to discuss is what the Gallup Leadership interview actually measures and whether more traditional and less expensive measures can be substituted.

Gallup proposes they are measuring a cluster of leadership personality traits. My area of specialization at the Ph.D. level was the area called personality. Well-accepted personality traits include introversion-

208

extroversion, field dependence-independence, and repression-sensitization. Dr. Hadfield uses the example of introversion-extroversion (I-E) in his talk. In fact I-E is a perfect example of a personality trait. It is stable over time (primarily genetic), it accurately predicts a person's response choices in a variety of situations, it is reasonably independent of other known traits such as ability or ability potential (IQ), and it is value neutral (i.e., being extroverted is not considered better than being introverted).

Let us now look at Gallup's leadership measure(s), which I will refer to as "L". One, according to Gallup, L is stable over time. This concept is obviously frustrating to people who want to teach leadership. However, it is essentially no different than measuring math potential. Some people score high and others low on mathematical ability. Everyone can still benefit from learning math. The high potential people will learn it faster and be able to go further with it (i.e., learn more difficult concepts).

Two, what behavior choices does L predict? If I know a person's score on I-E and he is given a choice of reading a book or attending a party, I can make a better than chance prediction. If you ask me which sports he prefers, I would have some idea as to whether he prefers team or individual sports. What behaviors can I predict given a person is high or low on L? The only thing I know about a high scorer on L is that he is likely to be similar to Corps people who were used as the criterion for creating L. Although this fact alone has some obvious value to the Corps, it is insufficient to qualify L as a trait.

Three, is L independent of other known traits? Let us first make sure that L is not just a circumlocutious measure of ability. There are at least two ways to assess this possibility. What Gallup will do is show you that their measure (L) predicts successful leaders. Certainly this is of prime importance. What Gallup will not show you is whether L predicts successful nonleaders. Consider the following possibilities:

Situation A

	Leaders		NonLeaders	
Successful	Yes	No	Yes	No
High L	80	20	50	50
Low L	20	80	50	50

Situation B

	Leaders		NonLeaders	
Successful	Yes	No	Yes	No
High L	80	20	80	20
Low L	20	80	20	80

In situation A, clearly L is a measure of leadership. In situation B, we are not sure what L measures but to call it leadership becomes problematic. Why would successful non-leaders score high on leadership? Why would they need leadership traits any more than baseball players need math ability?

Second, ask Gallup what the correlation is between L and any accepted measure of general mental ability (GMA). It is a well-known fact in the area of industrial psychology that a test of ability (such as work samples) or GMA is the best predictor of success in most occupations. A meta-analysis of over 32,000 employees "found that the validity of GMA for predicting job performance was .58 for professional-managerial jobs" ("The Validity and Utility of Selection Methods in Personnel Psychology: Practical and Theoretical Implications of 85 Years of Research Findings", Schmidt and Hunter, Psychological Bulletin, 1998, Vol. 124, No. 2, 262-274). Personality traits do have an impact on job success. In fact Schmidt and Hunter recommend a test of personal integrity to supplement GMA.

In the best of all worlds a GMA should be given to the criterion sample of successful leaders in the Corps. Dr. Hadfield mentioned the original sample was based on 1200 people of which 600 were in the "successful" group. What if GMA separated successful from unsuccessful leaders as well as L? What would you do? Test of General Mental Ability are easy to find and administer at low cost.

Four, is L value neutral? One of the differences between personality measures and ability or knowledge tests is that personality measures are usually value neutral. The Meyers-Briggs test classifies people into one of sixteen personality types. I have been to a leadership class where everyone took this test. I do not recall anyone complaining about having a "bad" personality type. On the other hand, most people want to score high on math or verbal ability, musical ability, or even tests of physical strength and speed. What about Gallup's measure(s) of leadership? Has anyone said, "I'm glad I am not one of those leadership types" or "Strategic thinking was something I never had an interest in."? I suspect that a lot of hostility is expressed toward Gallop's measure of L because a low score can seriously hamper one's career advancement. Consequently, people want to be able to improve their standing if they test in the lower tier. If L is truly a trait, then trying to score higher would be like scoring high on a test for schizophrenia and thinking your best move is to learn to answer the questions so as to appear less schizophrenic.

There is some advantage to trying to measure ability by looking for associated personality traits. Dr. Hadfield said that Gallup gets a subpoena about once per month. Unfortunately, the history of using a GMA for selecting applicants is even drearier in spite of the extensive literature in its support. I had actually devised a 30 item true or false test of statistical knowledge using items from a college introductory statistics book. I was advised by my Personnel Office not to use this test for screening applicants for a statistician position. Evidently basic knowledge of statistics had to be ascertained from transcripts and resumes. I know that not everyone is a good test taker but as Gallup loves to say, "This is not the sole criterion for selection." The Gallup measure of leadership might be the best the Corps can do to avoid being politically incorrect or in legal trouble.

Based on the current literature, my first proposition is that ability and ability potential are the best predictors of successful leaders. Successful leaders have to deal with volumes of information, systems, and people.

Leaders need to be knowledgeable on a variety of subjects. They must quickly absorb information, see relationships, discern causality and project the impact of a decision. Leadership under most conditions places a high value on both deductive and inductive reasoning.

On the other hand, we all know bright people who are awful leaders. What other factors are involved? A lot of leadership training classes emphasize interpersonal skills. Relationship is one of the leadership areas on the Gallup measure. I would guess that the 360 degrees evaluation used by the Corps would provide adequate information on interpersonal skills. Probably "likeability" (i.e., not being egotistical, authoritative, controlling, hostile) is important for leadership. Also leaders need to be good communicators. The ability to motivate people (salesmanship) is also important for leadership. Having empathy would be helpful when dealing with other people. Recent literature has demonstrated that women executives listen better, build consensus, and manage by personal influence more than men. According to Dr. Hadfield, men and women score equally high on L. It would be interesting to see how the average scores on the 20 talents (vision, concept, focus, ego drive, competition, achiever, courage, activator, relator, developer, multi-relator, individualized perception, stimulator, team, performance orientation, discipline, responsibility/ethics, arranger, operational, strategic thinking) vary by sex and race, statistics Gallup certainly has available.

What I would consider the third important area for leadership is interest. The Strong Vocational Interest test was one of the most useful tests I have ever taken. (It said my interests are like an entertainer/performer but that is another story.) I believe there exists a very simple way to test leadership interest – give people a choice of being promoted into a leadership or non-leadership position. This roughly translates into a supervisory or a technical position. I believe that a lot of our present leaders would have gladly stayed in technical positions if they could have received the same salary. Unfortunately this is a problem with most private and public organizations. Can you name any organization where a technical person can make as much money as the CEO? Allegedly Boeing Aircraft had a two-track system where managers and leaders followed one track and technical people followed another and neither track had any monetary advantage.

Down in fourth position is where I consider that value of personality traits relevant to leadership. Probably Gallup's "Drive to Execute" is the closest to being an actual trait. Simply put, intelligent people with good interpersonal skills and interests in leadership will vary in amount of drive. The people with a high needs to achieve will probably make better leaders under most situations. Never the less, isn't drive an important trait for success in just about any endeavor? Why would a leader need drive any more than a janitor to exceed in his or her field?

I agree with Dr. Hadfield from Gallup that who you need for any one position is situational specific. As he said, General Patton was good in war but not in peace. If the Corps way of doing business is shifting from stovepipes to programs and projects, do we need more leaders with relationship skills? I think it would be a good idea for the Corps to ask Gallup for the criteria that corporations use to select leaders. Dr. Hadfield, himself, indicated that different settings require different types of leaders. The Corps needs diversity among the top if only to be prepared for change. By diversity I am referring to personalities and points of view. Using the Meyers-Briggs test is one way to insure diversity. Top leaders should have a variety of personality profiles. I might add that situational factors were the very same arguments previously given by ability testers. For example, perhaps you should not hire the overall smartest person for an engineering designer position but the one who scores highest on spatial ability. A leader might need higher verbal skills than the typical engineer.

Lastly, there is the issue of values. Perhaps we can agree on honesty and dependability (like mom and apple pie) as being important in our leaders. However, what if we find that most successful leaders spend long hours on the job. Does this mean that good family men or women should be passed over? Psychologists have a test for everything and there is the Allport-Vernon Scale of Values if you want value diversity among leaders.

In summary, I recommend the following:

(1) Determine if Gallup measures leadership or a general measure of potential by identifying the most successful high-graded technical (non-leader) personnel from other high-graded technical people and having Gallup measure their leadership potential (without knowing who is in which group). Essentially see if situation A or B (see page 2) is closer to the truth.

(2) Correlate a test of general mental ability with Gallup's measure of leadership.

(3) Obtain from Gallup the criteria of leadership for other non-corps groups.

I believe the Gallup measure of leadership is just one of many ways of improving the quality of future leaders in the Corps of Engineers. However, it is important that you fully understand the process. The good old boy system of promotion was criticized for keeping the same type of people at the top. The Gallup Corporation has refined this process but it is still a selection based on "more of the same" and not based on independent performance measures (e.g., company profits, congressional funding). Furthermore, the Gallup process claims to measure a cluster of leadership traits or talents "distinct from skills or competencies" (The Gallup Leadership Profile handout).   This is at best a half-truth. Nine of the twenty leadership "talents" begin with the phrase "The capacity to" or "The ability to" (ibid). I do not doubt for a moment that the results of Gallup interviews add value to the decision process of a selection panel. This information might even compensate for the individual prejudices of panel members. However, given the time and the cost of the Gallup, there are other traditional selection procedures that might yield a better cost/benefit ratio. Unfortunately, the tried and true measurement of ability with work samples or knowledge tests and the measurement of ability potential with the use of general mental ability exams are not politically correct at this time. Consequently a nebulous leadership measure may be ideal because it is most likely to be upheld in court.

Appendix 8

SHARED INTERESTS
Copyright 1998, J. Alexander Wieriman

Would you like to meet someone who is good looking, intelligent, rich, honest, dependable, sensitive, and affectionate? Who wouldn't! On the other hand, not everyone is looking for someone who loves to attend the theater when not out fishing. Shared Interests was created to bring you in touch with persons who like what you like. Your lifestyle is unique.

Singles will be matched with five people of the opposite sex having shared interests. Unlike dating services, **Shared Interests can also put couples in touch with each other.** Matches will not deviate more than one Age Group from the applicant's.

Please fill out the following information about yourself (or as a couple):
Last Name: _ _ _ _ _ _ _ _ _ _ _ _ _ _ _ _ _
First Name(s): _ _ _ _ _ _ _ _ _ _ _ _ _ _ _ _ _ _ _
Address: _
City: _ _ _ _ _ _ _ _ _ _ _ _ _ _ _ _
State: _ _   Zip Code: _ _ _ _ _   _ _ _ _
Telephone Number: (_ _ _) _ _ _ - _ _ _ _
Status: __ Single   __ Couple
Sex: __ Male __ Female
Age Group: __ 18-25 __ 26-35 __ 36-47 __ 48-61 __ 62+
Ethnicity: __ White __ Black __ Hispanic __ Asian __ Other
Education in Years (12=High School, 16 = College): _____

217

Read the entire booklet and select up to ten of your favorite interests. List them in your order of preference.

INTERESTS

_ _ _ First Preference   _ _ _ Sixth Preference

_ _ _ Second Preference   _ _ _ Seventh Preference

_ _ _ Third Preference   _ _ _ Eighth Preference

_ _ _ Fourth Preference   _ _ _ Ninth Preference

_ _ _ Fifth Preference   _ _ _ Tenth Preference

As SHARED INTERESTS is not able to personally screen the many applicants we receive, we rely on your discretion when contacting others.

SPORTS
111 Football
112 Baseball
113 Basketball
114 Hockey
121 Soccer
122 Rugby
123 Track & Field
124 Gymnastics
125 Volleyball
131 Boxing
132 Wrestling
133 Judo/Karate
141 Tennis
142 Racquetball
143 Badminton
151 Golf
161 Downhill Skiing
162 Cross-country
......Skiing
171 Horse Racing
172 Auto Racing
181 Fencing

OUTDOORS
211 Bird Hunting
212 Game Hunting
213 Fresh Water
......Fishing
214 Salt Water
......Fishing
215 Riflery/Guns
216 Archery
221 Camping
222 Hiking
......Backpacking
223 Climbing
224 Spelunking
225 Bird Watching
226 Picnics
231 Dogs
232 Cats
234 Birds
235 Fish
236 Other Pets
237 Wildlife/Zoos
241 Vegetable
......gardening

242 Flower
......gardening
243 Landscaping
244 Farming
251 Canoeing
252 Boating
253 Sailing
254 Kayaking
255 Skin/Scuba
......Diving
256 Waterskiing
257 Surfing
261 Automobiles
262 Motor/Trail
......biking
263 Recreation
......Vehicles
271 Flying/Piloting
272 Skydiving
273 Hang Gliding
274 Ballooning

HEALTH & FITNESS
281 Aerobics
282 Exercise
......weights
283 Running
......Jogging
284 Bicycling
285 Swimming
......Diving
286 Walking
287 Massage
288 Yoga
291 Nutrition &
......Health
292 Vegetarianism
293 Holistic
......Medicine
294 Stress
......Management

HOBBIES
311 Handicrafts
312 Sewing/Clothes

313 Knitting/Crochet
314 Weaving
315 Silk Printing
316 Ceramics
317 Jewelry/Gems
318 Woodworking
319 Leatherwork
321 Photography
322 Videotaping
323 Drawing
......Painting
324 Calligraphy
325 Sculpturing
326 Flower
......Arranging
331 Interior
......Decorating
341 Mechanics
342 Electronics
343 Amateur Radio
344 Home Repair
351 Personal
......Computers
361 Astronomy
371 Model Building
372 Model
......Railroading
381 Remote control
......toys

COLLECTING
390 Stamps
391 Coins
392 Books
393 Records
394 Antiques
395 China/Glass
396 Dolls
397 Toys
398 Gems/Fossils
......Shells
399 Butterflies
......Insects

GAMES
411 Bowling
412 Pool/Billiards
413 Horseshoes
414 Croquet
415 Shuffleboard
416 Table Tennis
417 Darts
421 Various Card
......Games
422 Bridge
423 Poker
424 Pinnacle
425 Bourre
426 Bunko
431 Board Games
432 Knowledge
......Games
433 Word Games
......Puzzles
434 Chess
435 Backgammon
436 Strategy Games
437 Electronic
......Games
438 Fantasy Games
441 Social Games
442 Charades
443 Picture Games
451 War Games
......(Acted)
461 Magic
471 Bingo
472 Contests
473 Treasure Hunts
474 Casino
......Gambling
475 Lotteries
481 Making Money
482 Stock Market

LEISURE
511 Cooking
512 Baking
513 Restaurants
......Dining
514 Wines
521 Television
522 Radio
523 Movies
524 Reading
531 Drama
......Historical
532 Soap Operas
533 Comedy
534 Suspense
......Crime
535 Action
......Adventure
536 Horror
537 Science Fiction
538 Non-fiction
541 Freestyle
......Dancing
542 Ballroom
......Dancing
543 Country
......Dancing
544 Cajun Dancing
545 Square/Folk
......Dancing
551 Parties/Social
552 Nightclubs
......Lounges
553 Carnival (Mardi
......Gras)
554 Circuses
......Carnivals
561 Family
......Gatherings
562 Diner Parties
563 Visiting
571 Roller Skate or
......Blade
572 Ice Skate
581 Travel/Trips
582 Sightseeing
583 Walking Tours
584 Cruises
585 Cities
586 Historical Sites
591 Auctions
592 Shopping
593 Fashions

PROFESSIONAL
611 Physics
......Chemistry
612 Geology
613 Botany
614 Zoology
615 Medicine
......Biology
616 Mathematics
617 Computer
......Science
618 Engineering
619 Architecture
621 Social Sciences
622 Geography
......Cultures
623 Humanities &
......Literature
624 History
625 Law
626 Politics
627 Journalism
628 Education
629 Philosophy
......Religion
631 Business
......Economics
632 Management
633 Sales/Marketing
634 Manufacturing
641 Fine Arts
651 Languages
661 Military
671 Agriculture
681 General
......Education
682 College
......Preparation
683 Career Planning
691 Current Events
692 Futurism

REGIONAL
711 German
712 French
713 Italian
714 Greek
715 Slavic
716 Scandinavian
717 Russian
721 Hispanic
731 African
741 Asian
751 Mid-Eastern
761 Native
......American
771 New Orleans
......& LA
781 Genealogy

ARTS
811 Classical
......Music
812 Easy Listening
......Music
813 Rock/Pop
......Music
814 Country Music
815 Folk Music
816 Jazz
817 Opera
818 Singing/Choir
819 Band
......Instrumental
821 Songwriting
......Composing
831 Theater/Drama
832 Dinner Theater
833 Poetry
841 Writing
......Publishing
851 Visual Arts
852 Museums
861 Ballet/Dance
871 Clowning
881 Puppets
......Marionettes

RELIGION
911 Catholicism
912 Protestantism
913 Judaism
914 Islam
915 Eastern
......Religions
921 Metaphysics
......Occult
922 Astrology
923 Dreams

SERVICE
931 Community
......Service
932 International
......Service
933 Church Work
934 Conservation
......Ecology
935 Youth Work
936 Scouting
937 Children's
......Sports
941 Illness &
......Rehab.
942 Mental Health
943 Alcohol &
......Drug Abuse
944 Mental
......Retardation
945 Corrections
951 Student Issues
952 Race Issues
953 Senior Citizen
......Issues
954 Gay Issues
945 Women's
......Issues
951 Republican
......Party
952 Democratic
......Party
953 Other Parties

FICTITIOUS REPLY EXAMPLE

Applicant

April 21, 1999

Applicant: Richard Jones   Telephone: (504) 555-5555
Status: Single   Sex: Male   Age Group: 18-25
Ethnicity: White   Education (yrs): 14   Zip: 70118

Rank	Interest	Rank	Interest
1.	Archery	6.	Coins
2.	Jazz	7.	Physics/Chemistry
3.	Football	8.	Bicycling
4.	Baseball	9.	Nightclub/Lounges
5.	Basketball	10.	Movies

First Match

Respondent: Jennifer Altman   Telephone: (504) 555-5555
Status: Single   Sex: Female   Age Group: 18-25
Ethnicity: White   Education (yrs): 12   Zip: 70124

Rank	Interest	Rank	Interest
1.	Archery	6.	Aerobics
2.	Jazz	7.	Movies
3.	Ballet	8.	Restaurants/Dining
4.	Bicycling	9.	Gymnastics
5.	Ballroom Dancing	10.	Baseball

Second Match

Respondent: Paula Martinez   Telephone: (504) 555-5555
Status: Single   Sex: Male   Age Group: 26-35
Ethnicity: Hispanic   Education (yrs): 16   Zip: 70115

Rank	Interest	Rank	Interest
1.	Archery	6.	Coins
2.	Restaurants/Dining	7.	Classical Music
3.	Photography	8.	Jazz
4.	Basketball	9.	Travel/Trips
5.	Mathematics	10.	Youth Work

I believe my concept of "Shared Interests" is still valid. While the major matching service will link up men and women, *Shared interests* will link couples with couples. The potential is there for linking up same-sex people for friendship.

My list of interests is copyrighted but if you contact me (jalex1717@outlook.com), I will give you the right to use this list for the metropolitan area in which you live. Of course you are free to update the list of interests.

The entire concept is done by a data base and queries. I will also send you the Access database that I developed.   There exists several software packages for creating a website. You will need one that handles a database. You will only need the data processing skills necessary for this limited area of application or you might contract that service. Once developed, you will only need regular backups and maintenance.

Appendix 9

Book Review

J. Alexander Wieriman

My career path was unique. With the hundreds (thousands?) of Amazon e-books out there, I will bet you that I am the only one who requested Amazon to drop a customer review of my book "Counseling: A Profession or a Trade?" because it was too favorable. After several years with no comments from my limited number of customers, someone finally created the following review:

By Joshua T on November 10, 2015
Verified Purchase
This is a superb book, and I am amazed that it is languishing without a single review prior to mine. I have a BA and MA in psychology obtained in the sixties, similar to the author, and agree with over 95 percent of his views (without his statistics background). Wieriman knows the theory and practice of many of the therapies used over the last half century, how they relate to each other, and how they work (or mostly do not) in counseling. His writing is based on much management and measurement experience, and is generally insightful and frequently humorous. His major thesis is that therapy at best sets specific goals and measures progress towards them, and that, for this, a well-trained technician who can relate well to people is adequate for everything except prescribing medication. Advanced degrees, authoritarian presentation and speech, and fancy theories come under what he calls the "shamanism" effect, and are fine for people who need them in order to trust a counselor, but Wieriman doesn't think they add much to effective change in a client apart

from their placebo effect.

The book is much richer than this, and, for a mere three dollars in Kindle, is a must read for any intellectually honest person in the social services or mental health field.

I know that if I had read this review, I would think that the author wrote it and had one of his friends buy the book and post this. If this wasn't my only review, it would probably have helped me a lot. As it was it halted the sale of my book.

Of course, Amazon responded that they could not remove my review as it did not violate their posted guidelines.

Appendix 10

Cultural Change – What is it?

General Flowers talked a lot about changing our culture. One of the last things he said before retirement was "In my mind, it is absolutely critical to the nation to have a Corps of Engineers that it can turn to. So we owe it to those who came before us, and owe it to those who we serve, to change our culture." (ENGINEER UPDATE, July 2004). While a lot has been said about changing our culture over the last couple of years, I have not seen anyone define exactly what this means. Although I am not an anthropologist, I would like to give you my take on what I believe is cultural change and what is not.

First, I think it is easier to say what is not cultural change.

Proposition 1: We will always have a sizable number of people who do not like change.

We all know who these people are. They eat supper at 6 P.M. everyday. They always eat turkey on Thanksgiving. They have found a style of dress they like and they stick to it. These people are the salt of the earth. They find out how to do their jobs and they do it well. They are comfortable with the way things are. They do not like change. Cultural change has no special meaning for them over any other kind of change.

Proposition 2: Some people are skeptical of big changes based on past experience.

In one Dilbert cartoon, Dilbert is being told by his boss that they are reorganizing. Dilbert asks if that means the previous three reorganizations were failures. A lot of proposed changes are based on noble ideas without well-defined milestones and measures of success. General Ballard proposed "One door to the Corps." I thought it would be great if someone who wanted information from the Corps could call one number and not get referred elsewhere. My idea of "One door to the Corps" has not happened.

Proposition 3: New technology is seldom a cultural change.

I remember when we first got computers on our desks. A lot of people thought they should get a grade increase for learning a new skill. (If a computer makes your job easier should you get a grade decrease?) The use of personal computers was a major revolution but was not a cultural change unless you were Amish. Likewise, the use of P2 would not qualify as a cultural change. Neither is video-teleconferencing. Ever since Henry Ford, our culture likes to use machines to help us do our work.

So what is cultural change?

Proposition 4: Cultural change is a change in the informal unwritten expectations and behavioral patterns we demonstrate.

A good example would be a young married couple with children. It would be perfectly logical for the spouse with the most marketable skills to work while the other spouse stayed home to care for the children. If we followed this logic instead of the unwritten rules of our culture there would certainly be a lot more husbands at home.

I think the openness of information in the Corps is a cultural change for many people. In the past, people had their own private desk in their own department and assumed privacy was a right. Today we are reminded regularly that our personal computer is not personal at all but the property of the federal government. OMBIL allows us to view how the cost/benefits of our project line up with others across the nation. Likewise, General Flowers warned us against protecting our "fiefdom". Virtual teaming reminds us that we are one Corps. To say one Corps district is better than another would be like telling our left hand that our right hand is better.

I don't think the idea of the Corps as a learning organization is particularly new. We have always had on-going training and Individual Development Plans. The Corps has often been recognized as innovative. Furthermore, the project team approach has been around forever, although I believe we are expanding its boundaries. What has been a cultural change, at least for where I work at Waterborne Commerce Statistics Center, is the concept that anyone can be a team leader and the leader can be a lower grade than many of its members. Also, with teams and virtual teams, the role of supervisor has changed and some assumptions about what a supervisor should be could constitute cultural change. For example, it may now be acceptable for a supervisor to know less about a subject matter than his or her subordinates. (Please send no jokes about this one!)

Another potential cultural change for the Corps is the full realization that we do what Congress wants. Consequently, environmental groups are not necessarily our adversaries. Saving coastal wetlands can be engineering as easily as building locks and dams.

So overall, I do believe the Corps is undergoing cultural changes. However, I also believe that the term is more of a buzz-word than a reality.

Appendix 11

Names – A Comic Monologue

As Shakespeare put it, one of our most important possessions is our name. Only you don't get to pick it. Your parents probably agonized over picking a name for you. There is the old reliable "junior", a book of baby names, relatives, and true creativity.

There is an episode on "The Simpsons" where Homer has to pick a name for his son. He doesn't want it to rhyme with anything bad so he chose Bart. Children can be very creative when it comes to teasing you about your name. There's Bob the slob, Bert the Jerk, Doug the slug, Jane the pain. And God help you if your last name is Tucker.

Here is a hint – don't ever name a girl Katherine. People will never remember if it is spelled with a "K" or a "C". Then there is Jon. If he's old throw in an "h". There is Toni with an "i" and Tony with a "y". Some people deliberately mess with a name like naming a girl "Merry" as in Christmas.

Here is another hint. Do not give your child a name that could be either male or female like Chris, Carol, Pat, Connie, or Marion. Marion Morrison knew enough to change his name to John Wayne.

Some people like to name their child after someone famous such as George Washington Carver. Just about every nationality names women Mary. Why is it that the Mexicans are the only ones with the nerve to name their boy Jesus? Johnny Cash wrote a song called "A boy named Sue". The dad wanted his son to be tough. I have a suggestion. You want your boy to be tough. How about naming him Judas?

Down South people like to give their children two names like Jim Bob, Billy Ray or Betty Sue. I don't know how this tradition got started. I think they gave them two names in case they forgot one of them.

Of course there are parents who believe their child deserves a unique name. Do you ever read the badges of grocery clerks? Lots of original names there. Usually you have to guess at the pronunciation. The newspaper had a story about a lady who put a dash in her name. She said it was part of the pronunciation as in Kardashian. The singer Prince wanted a number in his name. I say if you want a number for a name, do it the old fashioned way – commit a crime.

No matter what your given name is you will probably have a nickname. The most common nickname is a short version of your name. Edward will become Ed, Susan will become Sue, Gregory will become Greg, and David becomes Dave. I have a simple suggestion. Why not just name your child Ed instead of Edward. He's going to be called that his whole life except when he is born, baptized, gets married and when he dies.

To complicate matters there is what the romance languages call the diminutive. First we shorten Edward to Ed and then we call him Eddy. Go figure. There is Johnny,

Jenny, Barry, Bennie, Willy, Winnie, Larry and Lenny. In theory the diminutive should only last through childhood. You know like Johnny Carson, Larry King and Billy Crystal.

Then we have the descriptive nickname. They say something about the person like Shorty, Moose, Speedy, Slim or Lucky. A few nicknames are ironic like Tiny. Have you ever known a "Tiny" who wasn't huge? They say the American Indians used descriptive names. One young Indian boy asked his father how he got his name. The father said "When your brother was born I saw an eagle so I named him "Flying Eagle". When your sister was born I saw a young fawn so I named her "Dancing Deer". Why do you ask "Stepping in Dog Crap"?

The strangest nicknames are those that do not appear to have any relationship to the original name. For example, suppose you name is Elizabeth. I will call you Liz, I will call you Beth, but don't ask me to call you Betty. Where did that come from? And why would someone named John go by Jack any more than someone named Jack would go by John? It makes no sense.

What really boggles my mind is a name that is shortened but changed. For example, the short form of William should be Will, not Bill. The short form of Robert should be Rob not Bob. Even Rebecca becomes Becky. What's with changing the first letter to a "B"? Fortunately, the short form of Mitchell is Mitch. The short form of Richard should be Rich. Who wouldn't want to be rich? I would like to be rich. On the other hand, how many of you guys would like to be a Dick? I didn't think so. Speaking of Dick, do you know anyone name Peter who doesn't insist on being called Pete? When former governor of Louisiana Huey Long got out of law school he thought of joining a law firm called Peters and Strong. However, he didn't think "Peters, Strong and Long" would work.

Appendix 12

Letters to the Editor

My best "letter to the editor" was published in 1995 and is as follows:

Change the Sentencing Process

For all its shortcomings. I believe the U.S. judicial system is one of the best in the world. Especially strong are our presumptions of innocence and a right to a trial by one's peers. Equally commendable is the legal system's strong rules for what constitutes admissible evidence.

If any changes need to be made, however, I believe it is in the sentencing process. After great pains to determine guilt or innocence, sentencing depends too much on the mood of a particular judge. All too easy prejudice can enter at this point. Is the accused remorseful? (Unfortunately, people wrongly accused are rarely remorseful.) Did the incident occur under a moment of passion or was it planned? Was the accused under the influence of alcohol or drugs?

Certainly judges should do the sentencing for minor offenses. I believe the disposition of serious crimes should be imposed by a panel of experts. These people can review the circumstances of the crime, the person's past history, present psychological state and the resources of the community. They can also balance each other's prejudices to produce a fair determination.

In line with the above recommendation is that juries should only determine guilt or innocence. They should not have to determine if a murder is first degree, second degree or manslaughter. Nor should they have to deal with whether the person committing the crime was insane or mentally deficient.

Juries should not have to worry about to what future they are condemning a person. If parole boards can determine if people are ready for release, certainly another board can determine what disposition is best for society.

Although not a letter to the editor, I believe that each state should have a pool of trial lawyers. For every trial, the prosecution chooses a lawyer and the defense chooses a lawyer. Then they are <u>randomly</u> assigned so the chosen lawyers may be working the opposite side. Consequently, if the defense can only afford a "public defender" priced lawyer, chances are the prosecution will match that. A person with money can still hire a team of lawyers to assist in his or her defense but may find themselves in court with a lawyer chosen by the prosecution. The best lawyers who do well on either side will likely be chosen for the most serious cases. Obviously the prosecution and defense will work together is deciding which lawyers to choose.

My funniest "letter to the editor" is:

David Brooks has shown us several ways to improve our economy. One of the simplest solutions is "if you take a two-earner high school-educated couple and get them college degrees, their income goes up by $58,000" (*Times-Picayune*, October 26). This seems to be short sighted. If this couple become physicians, their income goes up $158,000. If they do not like medicine, a Ph.D. in chemistry or petroleum engineering should also do the trick.

Appendix 13

The Dangers of Arbitrary Targets

Published in the *Federal Times*, August 11, 2014

J. Alexander Wieriman

The scandal at the Veteran's Administration (VA) hospitals is serious and widespread. Why would people cover up the wait times of veterans in need of medical attention? After reading the VA's yearly Performance Overview, it became clear that the VA is a big believer in targets. After attending a seminar by W. Edwards Deming and studying Statistical Process Control years ago, I became aware of the dangers of arbitrary targets. Let me begin with an example.

Suppose I am speaking with the Safety Director of a large company. He tells me his target is to reduce accidents by 20 percent this year. My first response is "I thought your target would be zero accidents". He replies of course that is his real goal but it is unrealistic. So I ask "Why do you think reducing accidents by 20 percent is realistic? Did they increase your budget by 20 percent? Did you recently discover a way to reduce accidents that was not known the previous year?" Of course he cannot answer "yes" to either of those questions. However, he does plan on putting safety posters in all of the elevators even though he knows of no studies that show this to be effective. So his last effort is to put me on the defensive.

He says targets give people an incentive to do well. How could they hurt?

Fortunately I have an answer for that. First, you should know your job well enough that you do not need targets. The Safety Director's full-time job is to reduce accidents. If he needs additional incentives to perform, I would replace him tomorrow. That does not mean I would not give bonuses to people who save the company money. However, I would not dangle money in front of anyone as an incentive. As far as the typical employee goes, I would hope that preventing a sprained back or a broken arm is incentive enough to concentrate on safety.

Second, targets give people an incentive to cheat. If your target is to reduce accidents by 20 percent and you are able to reduce them by 18 percent, what is the first thing you will do? You will probably look at all of the accidents to see if perhaps a few of those were "misclassified". By making a few corrections, you will have achieved your goal. Aren't most people honest? Do you know that most students, 70% to 95%, admit to cheating. The students will tell you that they cheated so they can get good grades to get into college and/or pacify their parents. A few students cheat because they are paid by their parents for every 'A' and 'B' they get. Let's hope the VA does not offer bonuses to managers who achieve their targets.

Honest people look for loopholes – think derivative funds. I know of a school that sent their "special" students on a field trip the day of testing so their school could achieve high scores. I heard of highway maintenance workers who were rewarded for not wasting paint. They carefully discarded any extra paint to achieve their goal. People find creative ways to meet targets.

A third problem with targets is that you will often achieve one target at the expense of another. In education this is known as teaching to the test. Let's suppose that the VA sets a target of seeing 50 % of their clients within 30 days. Suppose you are in charge of scheduling patients and you have a cancellation. You can either move up a client who is scheduled to be seen in 32 days from his first contact or a client who has been waiting six months to see a doctor. Moving the first client up helps you achieve your target of seeing clients within 30 days. Moving up the client who has been waiting for six months does not help you at all in achieving your target. So which person do you move up? Even worse, suppose a new administrator creates a policy of seeing persons first who have been waiting the longest. A year later you now have a chart that shows nobody was seen within 30 days.

The fourth reason targets are bad is that achieving a target does not guarantee you that things have actually improved. Every year our newspaper publishes crime statistics. When crime goes down, law enforcement takes credit. When crime goes up, we blame it on an influx of drugs beyond our control. Every process has normal variation. The number of murders that take place in a large city can vary widely from year to year. It is unlikely that a drop or increase in murders in any one year can reliably indicate anything. Statisticians doing quality control use a technique called "Statistical Process Control" to determine if the variation observed, such as the length of a widget, is normal or if the process is "out of control" based on observations over time. Statistical Process Control tells you if something special, good or bad, is happening. Furthermore, any statistician can measure if the VA hospitals significantly differ from each other on any reliable statistic such as age of clientele, length of treatment, cost per person, wait time, etc.

For the above reasons, I recommend the VA set no arbitrary targets such as the percent of clients seen within X number of days. Their goal will always be to see people as soon as possible. I recommend they give their complete data to a statistician who will give you the probability that any real change has occurred over time. The best graph for their Performance Overview would be the distribution of clients by days waiting to be seen. However, I would settle for the median and mean wait times. The median will tell you that half of the clients are seen within X number of days. The difference between the median and mean wait time will give you an indication of how many veterans are waiting months to see a doctor.

The VA hospitals will need to make many significant changes to improve. Getting rid of arbitrary targets will be the easiest. This will also free up a lot of people's time fixing things that are not broke, that is, targets not met as the results of normal variation.

Appendix 14

Cooking Lobsters

Why Things Get Worse Before They Get Better

J. Alexander Wieriman

We have all heard that by raising the temperature little by little, a lobster becomes a meal without realizing what is happening. My premise is that the most serious issues we have to face are those that creep up on us and we do not act until they become crises. Some of these issues include:

Federal Deficit

Personal Debt

Immigration

Collapse of Infrastructure

Obesity

Divorce

Crime

War

Global Warming/Oceans rising

Pollution

Poor Health

Axiom 1: We are genetically programmed to respond to immediate threats to our survival.

Corollary 1: People who solve problems get a lot more recognition than people who prevent them.

Rescuing a drowning person from a flood makes you a hero. Saving a thousand people from flooding by effective flood control gets you no recognition at all. People who handle crises rise up in the ranks. Being the mayor of New York during the September 11th crisis places you in contention to run for a higher office. Twelve U.S. presidents were generals. People remember war-time presidents. What would be the status of Abraham Lincoln if it were not for the Civil War? FDR is well known because of the Great Depression. Eisenhower became president as the result of being a general during World War II. As a president he was often referred to as the "do nothing" president. However, during his administration he created the interstate highway system that probably created more wealth than any other president. This wealth was generated long after he was in office when trucking took over the railroads as the chief means of product distribution. I would like to say that Eisenhower showed great foresight. Actually, he created the national highway system under the concept of defense. By law, most of the interstate system must be straight so that an airplane can land on it.

Rule 1 (The Cardinal Rule): It is better to prevent a crisis than to solve one.

This rule requires little explanation. Crises are costly. If you wait until that mole on your back become skin cancer you will have wished you had it removed earlier. An ounce of prevention is worth a pound of cure. When you look at a crisis in terms of dollars, this aphorism is an understatement. For example, by not following its own safety rules, BP had to spend over a billion dollars correcting an oil spill in the Gulf of Mexico. By not keeping down the federal deficit, we now pay millions in interest.

Axiom 2: Men fight wild beasts and each other; women raise children, gather food and prepare meals. In other words, men are programmed to respond to immediate danger while women need to prepare for the future.

Corollary 2: Men (or women like men) should carry out and enforce the plans that women (or men like women) make.

Prediction 1: The first woman president of the United States will have all of the characteristics of a man. In other words, she will not be the type of leader we need.

Rule 2: Unless there is a crisis, put a planner in charge.

Most captains of industry are still men and the United States is one of the few industrialized nations to have never had a woman in charge as president. We elect generals (12) and lawyers (25) to our highest office. These are people who see the world in an adversarial way. Voters like strong take-charge leaders. Women are more likely to rule by consensus. It may take longer to reach decisions by consensus but implementing them becomes easier.

Axiom 3: Maturity is the ability to delay immediate gratification for greater long-term gains.

Corollary 2: Leaders take credit for short-term gains and blame the previous leader for long-term problems.

Most CEO's are interested in making gains while they are still in charge. Stockholders want to see results quarterly. Consequently, most people do not consider maturity to be a desirable trait for a leader. We want what we want and we want it now!

I remember when young people lived in an apartment before they bought their "starter home". At that time the average home was about 1400 square feet. Now it is about 2400 square feet. The housing collapse of

2009 was fueled by people who over-bought with the encouragement of realtors and bankers.

Axiom 4: Consensus through diversity is an effective way to come up with the best solution to a problem.

Many studies have demonstrated that the decisions of a group exceed the decisions of any one individual for complex problems. Manager training seminars often ask people to choose what they need to survive in a hostile climate such as the desert or the arctic. When the group works together to reach a consensus to a problem they invariably do better than the solutions of individuals.

Corollary 4: Diversity as practiced by most businesses is not diversity at all.

If you want to create a diverse group, you need to first decide on what dimensions the group should differ on and then measure people. A group consisting of individuals of different sex, color, or national origin guarantees nothing! If you are not sure how to measure diversity for selection to a committee, I would suggest you have the candidates each take the Myers-Briggs Type Indicator test. This test classifies people into one of 16 personality types. The test rates people on the four dimensions of introversion-extraversion, sensation-intuition, thinking-feeling, and perceiving-judging. To insure a diversity of opinion, make sure that each person on the committee has a different personality type.

Axiom 5: The smaller the organization, the more efficient it is.

We all know about the problems with large bureaucracies. Too many levels of management with upper management too far removed from the day to day operations. Furthermore, bureaucracies have lots of committees that produce too many rules and regulations. Recently, the countries of the world were rated as to the best places to live based on health, education, and business climate. The top rated countries were all small!

Corollary 5: It is the nature of organizations to continually expand until they fall by their own weight.

Wal-Mart has destroyed small town businesses that cannot compete with the large discounts they get as the result of their size. **The fact that Wal-Mart can sell goods for less because of these discounts does not make them efficient.** Many a company has gotten rich from gobbling up smaller companies. The reason small companies exist at all is because they are usually more efficient and quicker to take action. Innovation can occur rapidly in a small company. General Motors was not the first to produce efficient cars when they were in demand or SUV's when the public wanted those. Fewer layers of bureaucracy and personal service will always allow small companies to compete.

Axiom 6: We take action when a problem reaches the breaking point.

Some breaking points are clear cut. When a bridge collapses we realize we need to put more effort in inspecting our bridges and making repairs. Having a number of bridges on the verge of collapse doesn't do the trick. No one gets credit for preventing a crisis. When people die we take notice. Most breaking points are vague. How many illegal immigrants do we need to have before this problem becomes a priority?

Corollary 6: We will always need problem solvers in charge if we never have planners to keep crises from happening in the first place.

Solutions to cooking lobsters

Action Points:

The simplest way to avoid the tremendous loss from creeping problems is to define an "action point". For example, suppose you are a person who constantly worries about your weight. The way to reduce your worries is to decide to take action if ever your weight exceeds a certain number. Once a month you should weigh yourself and if you are below the action point you forget about your weight until the next month. There is a method called Statistical Process Control (SPC) that can help you decide when a system is "out of control". SPC is one of the reasons for the tremendous strides the Japanese made in quality control after World War II. Quality control helped Toyota surpass GM in the number of automobiles sold in the world.

Our government should have action points. For example, taxes should automatically go up when X number of troops are deployed outside of the United States. This way we would pay as we go for military action instead of building up a huge debt. Some actions, such as retiree pay, are already tied to the Consumer Price Index. Minimum wages should also be tied to the Consumer Price Index. It would probably be a good idea if the treasury rate went up or down by a formula. That way a committee would meet only in cases when this formula needs to be over-ruled.

Proportional Response:

Proportional response requires a response in proportion to change that has taken place. For example, a weight gain of ten percent might require a ten percent reduction in your daily calorie intake. One of the problems with governing by catastrophe is that a catastrophe calls for drastic measures and drastic measures lead to public revolt.

Planned Replacement:

When I was young, someone told me to pay for my first automobile with cash. Then I should put a little money aside each month for my next car. That way I would never have to finance an automobile. When I worked in data processing for the United States government we paid for our data processing equipment with "Planned Replacement" funds. Whenever the government builds a bridge, they need to set aside a small amount of money for replacing or repairing that bridge.

Savings:

Clearly one of the best ways to save money is to avoid interest charges as pointed out above. Whenever someone asks me if I am for a balanced budget I always reply "no". After a few awkward stares I then explain that I am not for a balanced budget because I believe the government should take in more than it spends. I would still be living in a trailer if I spent every penny I ever made. As a nation the United States is not a believer in savings. Furthermore, our parents probably saved a greater proportion of their income than we do. Savings is nothing new. Moses had the Egyptians store grain for the bad years.

Rule 3: Create Long Term Goals:

Presidents are not believers in long term goals because they want to get credit for their actions while in office. The same goes for company CEO's. The way to get around this is for unelected committees to meet and work out long term goals. Term limits is another solution. Supreme Court justices have the options to go against public opinion. Public opinion will never favor long term goals. Too many people live from pay check to pay check. They do not want to put money aside for infrastructure, upgrading technology, and that proverbial rainy day.

Fortunately, every individual can put something aside, even if it is only pocket change. Putting a small amount aside that earns interest is invaluable, especially when you start this habit with your first job. So what if your friends think you are poor when you do not buy that house and car you can barely afford. It is only a matter of time before you pass them up.

Rule 4: Invest in Knowledge and Skills

Everyone needs basic skills in communication and problem solving. Some things are learned by having a formal education. Most skills, however, are passed down to you from someone else. Early generations put more of an emphasis on being a jack of all trades. They saved a lot of money by not hiring repairmen. Certain skills, such as cooking and carpentry, will always have value in the best and worst of times. How many older people have said they had wished they had learned to play piano when they were young?

Axiom 7: No one knows the value of a college education.

The only way to assess the value of a college education would be to randomly pick some people to go to college while others are randomly excluded from college. Without random assignments, studies that show college graduates make more money are meaningless. These studies do not even control for intelligence and social class.

Rule 5: Pick a Mate Who Shares your Long Term Goals

A grasshopper and an ant make a poor combination. Two ants do not go together any better when one ant loves the city and the other the country. Sharing values is important but it is not the same as sharing long term goals.

People without long term goals choose the best paying job and the best looking mate offered now. Choose the job, the location, and your partner that is the most compatible with where you want to be down the road and be patient.

Axiom 8: Follow your Dream but be Prepared First

Prediction 2: The National Debt will eventually create a financial catastrophe causing one of the largest Stock Market drops in history.

So What's for Dinner?

Appendix 15

Application for Employee Assistance Coordinator

J. Alexander Wieriman

Records Management

Accomplishments:

(1) Assisted Brainerd State Hospital in making a transition from a traditional medical department oriented record to a problem oriented record. That is, all transactions entered into the patient's file must reference a previously defined problem or goal.

(2) Single-handedly turned a manual system of tracking 18,000 army medical personnel into a fully automated database system with real-time updates, audit trails, validity checks, and automatic report generation. This new menu driven system saved approximately 500 man-hours per month and allowed for information retrieval impossible under the old system.

Proposals:

(1) With computer assistance, all Employee Assistance transactions (e.g., client information, services provided) would be recorded on a real-time basis.

(2) Eighty percent (80%) of all requests for information regarding the Employee Assistance Program would be immediately available from a menu driven system (i.e., a printer generated report).

In-service Training

Accomplishments:

(1) I was involved in the creation and opening of the Psychiatric Unit at Brainerd State Hospital. Consequently, we had many employees to train. I did all of the counselor training.

(2) Participated in the regional training of law enforcement officers for all of northern Minnesota.

(3) Developed several seminars for business and the general public. For example, through Joskes of Texas I taught classes on "Handling Tension" "Creative Problem Solving" and "Interpersonal Skills".

(4) Taught "Statistics for Business" at the University of Texas, San Antonio.

Proposals:

(1) Ascertain the talents already available among city employees to insure a sharing of knowledge.

(2) Make skill training sessions related to personal and social skills available to all city employees.

(3) Use a well-documented personal profile (PERFORMAX) along with job analysis to assist in the development of excellent working relationships among city employees.

Inter-Departmental Cooperation

(1) Was instrumental in breaking down the traditional hospital pyramid (i.e., psychiatrist, psychologist,

social worker, nurse, etc.) to establish a counselor based system. In other words, the specialized staff acted as consultants to the counselors. Note: Mental health organizations are notorious for giving the most power to those who know the least about the patient.

(2) As chairman of the Research Committee of Minnesota Psychologists in Public Service we embarked on an ambitious study of following patients discharged from state hospitals through the various state and local services such as county welfare and mental health clinics. One study involved pairs of psychologists from different facilities doing door to door follow-ups.

(3) Coordinated a two day conference on program evaluation for psychologists and hospital administrators throughout the state of Minnesota.

Proposals:

(1) Establish a monthly newsletter to keep department managers informed of Employee Assistance programs and items of special interest.

(2) Solicit suggestions on how the Employee Assistance Program can best meet the needs of the different city departments.

Program Evaluation

Accomplishments:

(1) Developed a system of evaluation for Brainerd State Hospital using three sources of information –

significant others, the clients, and hospital statistics such as readmission rates and workload indices. A standardized pre/post measure was filled out by a significant other such as a spouse or friend and the results were analyzed by computer. Due in large part to this system, Brainerd State Hospital was one of only seven multiservice hospitals nationwide to receive accreditation.

(2) Initiated an information/evaluation system for a two county correctional area as a pilot project for the Minnesota Community Corrections Act.

(3) Evaluated specially funded education programs such as basic skills, special education, math, and bilingual education for the Education Service Center, Region 20 (14 counties). I developed most of the evaluation instruments used. All technical reports began with a one page executive summary followed by a section on utilization of findings by project staff.

Proposals:

(1) Develop a program evaluation system using a least three sources of information. This system would be geared toward improving existing services.

(2) Work to create measures of cost effectiveness based on reducing absenteeism, saving retraining costs, etc.

(3) Make available my expertise in program evaluation as well as research and data analysis to other departments.

Management

Accomplishments:

(1) Administered a chemical dependency program for over three years. Directly under my supervision was one counselor and two VISTA volunteers. In addition, I shared a number of nursing staff.

(2) Was chairman for two years of the Research Committee of Minnesota Psychologists in Public Service. We undertook many cooperative studies.

(3) Worked with many project managers of educational programs helping them develop objectives and timelines.

(4) While at the Education Service Center I developed an assessment of how managers use information based on their level of "maturity".

Proposals:

(1) Follow an incentive driven program as opposed to one based on reprimands and fear of failure.

(2) Foster a spirit of equality and cooperation by viewing management as a function and not a position of superiority.

(3) Emphasize the Employee Assistance Coordinator's role as a facilitator.

Counseling

(1) While at Brainerd State Hospital I conducted individual, group, and family therapy using the usual methods of psychologists.

(2) Minimized inefficient "talk about your problems" groups in favor of role playing and skill training.

(3) Created my own cognitive therapy called "Semantic Readjustment". This method is based on the premise that one's beliefs structure one's experiences.

(4) Created and administered a chemical dependency program called "Time Structuring" based on social learning theory. I trained the counselor. This program received an award from the National Institute of Drug Abuse.

Proposals:

(1) Assuming the City of San Antonio has similarities to industry, alcohol and drug abuse prevention and treatment programs are probably the most cost effective employee assistance programs. It is necessary to insure that clients are matched to the appropriate program.

(2) Insure that all services available to city employees by referral are goal oriented and progress notes are kept.

(3) Keep a current file of resources within the San Antonio area with notes regarding experiences with each facility.

Appendix 16

Thoughts of an Independent

J. Alexander Wieriman

Introduction

Almost from its inception, the United States has had a two party system. Unlike many other countries, third parties have had a minimal impact on our political system. For most of our history the two dominant parties are republicans and democrats. The majority of voters and the overwhelming majority of candidates affiliate with one of these parties. People without a party affiliation are called independents. The primary reason that most candidates associate with either the Republican Party or the Democratic Party is that the party provides the means, which is money and manpower, to get elected. As any statistician can tell you it is unlikely that the philosophy of the masses would be bimodal. Clearly most people would be in the middle. However, do not get confused into thinking that an independent is therefore in the middle. An independent can hold some positions that are far right and far left at the same time.

Independents in Congress

With the republican and democratic parties evenly matched in congress, a representative of congress who is independent could weld great clout. He or she could make the difference on important legislation. Presently only two independents exist. I predict the number of independents in congress will increase as the result of the internet. First of all, a person running for office can reach a lot of people through the internet and vice-versa. People wanting to learn about a candidate can read their website. Second, the use of a computer program that lines up a voter with the candidate that best represents him or her will attract more voters. Two such websites were active during the election of 2008. I expect many of those voters who used one of those matching sites were surprised at who the computer said was most in line with their views. This could be especially embarrassing if that candidate was of a different party than their usual preference. In any case, I do not believe such broad labels as liberal and conservative are particularly informative. I think most people have a unique configuration of beliefs. That is what makes someone an independent. You are about to hear what my beliefs are on a number of important issues are.

Immigration

I thought I would follow with one of my two extremes. On immigration, my ideas would be considered to be far to the right. I asked myself, "What would keep me from coming to the United States if I were a poor Mexican?" My answer: I might come here illegally but I would not have children if I knew that even if they were born here, they would be sent to Mexico if my illegal status was <u>ever</u> discovered. So I suggest we change the law that that makes children who are born in the United States automatically citizens. Then we should verify that everyone attending our public schools is a United States citizen. Single people who come to the United States illegally are probably working at jobs that most people consider undesirable. *The key to immigration reform is to keep families from coming here (or starting here).*

As to the idea of securing our borders, I have one word for that – Canada. How much do you think it would cost to secure our border with Canada? Don't think Mexican drug lords with lots of money haven't already thought of that.

As to what to do with the thousands of illegal immigrants already here, I am open to suggestions. However, this is a side issue; not the important one.

The War of Drugs

If my views on immigration are far to the right, my views of drug abuse are far to the left. The war on drugs was started by Richard Nixon over 30 years ago and there is no end in sight. The principle reason for the failure of our war on drugs is that the battle is waged by politicians. Drug czars have been political appointments based on loyalty to the party. For starters, the United States has never had a sane rational for what drugs should be illegal. Let me explain this in an easy to understand manner.

(1) If the drug that caused the most damage in lives and dollars was illegal, alcohol would be illegal.

(2) If the drug that was the most addictive was illegal, cigarettes would be illegal.

(3) If the drugs that were most abused were illegal, prescription drugs would be illegal.

(4) If the drug most used disproportionately by minorities was illegal, cocaine would be illegal.

There is evidence that alcohol in moderation is healthy and marijuana can counteract the nausea of certain cancer medications. Cigarettes appear to be one of our most useless drugs contributing directly to over 150,000 deaths annually and indirectly to 400,000 more; way more than all of our other illegal drugs combined. The problem is political. *Smoking cigarettes will never be illegal simply because our society will never put a lot of teenagers and middle-aged white women in jail.*

By using the term drug war instead of addiction problem, we place our trust in the criminal justice system instead of health care. Even with this choice the money is used poorly. We give it to countries like Columbia. Equally dumb is to go after suppliers instead of users. Put a supplier in jail and another person takes his place. I have yet to hear the story of a user who took up drugs because someone was sent to jail.

As I see it there are three better solutions to our drug problem. Probably the least controversial approach is for our war on drugs to stay within the justice department but to focus our efforts on competing with the suppliers instead of trying to arrest them. By competing, I suggest the Federal Government could have a large number of undercover agents selling illegal drugs, both to individuals and to small dealers. However, these drugs being sold would have a small proportion tainted with pharmaceuticals that will make a person severely nauseous. It would be the equivalent of selling alcohol containing antabuse (disulfiram), a drug used in the treatment of alcoholism. *Drug users might go a long time before hitting a bad batch but when they do it will have lasting impact.* Most people I know will never return to a restaurant that gave them food poisoning, even if it was only one time out of ten.

The second possible approach to solving our drug problem is to place the use of all illegal drugs primarily under the health care system. Why not make the nonviolent possession of <u>all</u> illegal drugs, no matter the amount, a misdemeanor that avoids any fines or jail time if the person attends a treatment program? Many states already have special drug courts. However, we still spend enormous amounts of the taxpayers' money sending dealers and multiple offenders to jail for many years even though the emotional and financial costs of legal drugs such as alcohol and cigarettes far exceeds the costs of illegal drugs. Furthermore, a 1997 RAND study estimates that treatment reduces drug related crimes 15 times more than mandatory sentences.

Lastly, we could legalize all drugs used by adults. This does not mean we would not arrest people driving under the influence or fire people coming to work impaired. Would legalization increase the use of these drugs? Certainly, probably three fold. However, the damaging costs caused by these drugs, including treatment, would still result in an overall savings over our present system. As of the year 2000, the United States spends 24 billion dollars on the incarceration of nonviolent offenders, the bulk of which are drug offenses (Justice Policy Institute).

The best reason for legalizing drugs is that no one will consider any drug to be safe just because it is legal. Personally, I would include prescription drugs in this list. Any adult who wants to be his own doctor should be able to. Let the fools weed themselves out as nature intended.

Deficit Spending

The United States has both a huge deficit and a huge national debt. All of our politicians have known this for years. So why is nothing done? **The problem is not Congress. It is us.** Politicians know they cannot be elected or re-elected promising less for more. Walter Mondale wanted to deal with deficit spending when he ran for president. He lost 49 of 50 states. The first George Bush also wanted to correct the deficit. He lost his re-election. Simpson-Bowles had a plan. Nobody jumped on the bandwagon. Let's face the truth. We cannot change self-interest.

So what do I suggest? I suggest that every president and congressman serve a single term. I would go with five years for the president, eight years for a senator, and six years for a member of the House. This way a candidate can promises anything he or she wants but do something else once in office. The Supreme Court consistently gets higher approval ratings than the president or Congress and they are elected for life.

Taxes

Term limits might also help with simplifying our tax codes. If every politician knows that he or she cannot run for re-election they will be more inclined to do something for the general good, even if it offends some special interest group. We must do more than simply rewrite the code so everyone can understand it. There is no such thing as a "loophole". *Every page of the tax code exists because someone benefits from it.* Parents want tax deductions for their children. Rich people want a special capital gains rate. Home owners want to deduct their loan interest. The list goes on. Remember when we encouraged people to go into debt by allowing a deduction on credit card interest?

The problem with creating social and economic policy through taxes it that once something gets in, it rarely gets out. We can still reward special interests with grants that are time limited. Let's not do it with taxes. As every person has a special interest, I don't really see anything of importance happening in this area. Any suggestions? Note: The Simpson-Bowles Plan had a lot to say about taxes and was promptly ignored by both parties.

I recommend the following changes to our tax laws:

(1) Allow home buyers to deduct their mortgage interest for only 5 years.

(2) Allow charitable deductions only if the CEO makes less than $300,000 per year.
(3) Tax corporations at 25 percent with the following exceptions:
(A) Lower by 2% if they have profit sharing.
(B) Lower another 3% if they have loss sharing.
Note: Loss sharing saves the government from paying unemployment insurance.
(C) Raise the tax by .1% for every 1% of their workforce that are not U.S. citizens.
(4) Allow deductions for up to 4 dependents only.
(5) Do not allow landlords to take deductions for improvements to their property. They can recuperate the costs with rent increases.
(6) Do not ask anyone if he or she is married. Everyone who makes money should pay their own taxes.

Health Care

I think the only solution to health care is a two-tiered system. Those who can afford health care with the help of private insurance should continue to do so. The problem with insurance is that it is a profit making business. The best way to make a profit is to only insure the healthiest people. Consequently, we need a second public tier that provides health care to the poor. I suggest we create (or recreate) public hospitals like Veterans Administration hospitals. The government should pay for the education of doctors willing to spend four years after medical school staffing these public hospitals. These doctors would be paid a salary and would not have anything to do with the financial arm of the hospital. The military has used a similar approach. By paying for medical school, the doctors agreed to spend time in the armed services. It is a lot easier to manage a system with fixed buildings and equipment and with salaried workers than going the route of health insurance.

People on Medicare would be in the private tier until the money they and their employers contributed runs out. Then they would move on to the second tier. At the present time no one knows when his contributions to social security or Medicare have run out and the money he is receiving from the government is actually welfare. Money contributed to social security and Medicare should go into that proverbial lock box and every year you should get a statement, much like a retirement plan.

Both Social Security and Medicare were based on an expanding population supporting an older population. Given that is no longer the case, president Obama wanted the younger people without insurance to pay into a fund to support the elderly. No one should be forced to buy insurance. However, I do not see anything wrong with an emergency room not admitting people without insurance unless they sign over their automobile(s) to the hospital. If they cannot pay their bills within 90 days, the hospital can cash in the automobile(s) and refund any extra cash not needed for their bill. What makes this proposal eminently fair is that poor people have no cars or have a very inexpensive vehicle. This would make anyone with a $20,000 plus car wish they had bought insurance.

Appendix 17

Various Ideas of Mine

J. Alexander Wieriman

(1) I believe that psychiatry should be a specialty in pharmacology. I cannot understand making someone go through seven years of medical school so she can prescribe antidepressants and other psychotropic medications. Neurologists can deal with the medical aspects of a mental illness.

(2) I think that some people on welfare should live in a specially designed community that includes day care, schooling, medical assistance and work. Those refusing to move into the community would forgo their benefits. Of course the work should include training for a future job.

(3) I believe that companies should have loss sharing as well as profit sharing; that is, everyone should take a percent cut in pay before people get laid off. Salesmen on commission already work under similar conditions.

(4) I would like to see more independents in government. We need a special source of funding so they can compete with the major parties.

(5) I would like to see a flat tax or a national sales tax.

(6) I think that marriage should be a church functions and that the federal government does not need to know your marital status. Everyone who makes money should fill out one's own income tax form.

(7) We need an ongoing committee of scientists that will rank drugs (street drugs and prescription drugs) from 1 to 100 on their presently perceived value. A rating of "1" would be perfectly safe as well as valuable and a rating of 100 would mean certain death. Each state can then draw the line as to what is legal. However, if marijuana is rated lower (i.e., less destructive) than cigarettes, they can no longer make cigarettes legal and marijuana illegal.

(8) Prisons should be privatized with profits related to recidivism rates.

(9) Criminal judges should be civil service positions. What judge ever lost an election by being too harsh on criminals?

(10) It is difficult to know who to vote for in local elections when all you have are fliers. These are the prejudices I follow:

(A) Vote for anyone who does not show family members on their flier. I have applied for many jobs and have never shown a prospective employer pictures of my family.

(B) Rarely vote for any lawyers. Too many in politics already.

(C) Consider voting for anyone willing to support something controversial, even if I am against it.

(D) Vote for an independent.

(E) Rarely vote for anyone beyond a second term in office.

(11) It is time to rethink planned cities. Many of our huge cities located on a major body of water are in trouble when the oceans and rivers rise. Cities of over 3 million people have problems with infrastructure and transportation. Large cities cannot effectively evacuate from a hurricane. In 1975 the world had only three metropolitan areas with over 10 million people (New York, Tokyo and Mexico City). Today there are over 31 metropolitan areas with over 10 million people.

(12) What was wrong with Esperanto (or Spanish)? No one should need to know more than two languages.

(13) Someday someone is going to write a computer program that translates English into computer code. Note: This will make it difficult for foreigners without good English to compete.

(14) We need to change the spelling of ten words every year until our most common words are spelled like they sound. Spelling bees should be a thing of the past. I'll bet Spain doesn't have any.

(15)　We need to replace flood insurance with disaster insurance that covers natural disasters such as floods, tornados, forest fires, and earthquakes.

(16)　The government should cover the cost of terminal illnesses, such as Alzheimer's as verified by a committee of physicians.

(17)　U.S. mail service should be Monday, Wednesday and Friday.

(18)　Pennies cost more to produce than they are worth. When is the government going to stop making them?

(19)　The *Journal of the Endocrine Society* (November, 2017) concluded that sugar-sweetened drinks contribute to diabetes and metabolic syndrome. How about a national tax on sugary drinks?

(20)　Increasing our national tax on gasoline would also be a good idea. Rich people are more likely to have gas guzzlers and this would encourage the sale of electric automobiles.

(21)　The top 100 land owners own 40.2 million acres (more than the state of Florida). How about a limit on how much land a single person or corporation can own? Let's include a much smaller limit of land a foreigner can own.

Printed in Great Britain
by Amazon